A Practical Guide to Tourette's Syndrome for Parents in a Post-Pandemic World

Mandy M Barnett

First Printing: 2022

First published in 2022
Printed in the United Kingdom.
Compton Gray Books
A catalogue number for this book is available from the British Library

ISBN 978-1-7397784-0-8

Praise for It's NOT All About Swearing!

"I really wish my parents had read this growing up"

– Cece Jaye aka 'Otters Have Pockets'

A Note from Tourette's Action

"At Tourette's Action we want everyone with TS to receive the support and social acceptance they need to help them live their lives to the full. This book will educate you on what Tourette's actually is. It explains how to offer practical support and the importance of breaking down the stigma associated with TS."

– Emma McNally CEO Tourette's Action

10% of all author royalties are donated to Tourette's Action

Contents

Acknowledgements

I want to thank all the people who have helped me in writing this book.

My husband, Patrick James, for keeping everything else going so that I could write!

Our children, Alex James and Angelica James, for all their talented quirky individuality and for being the inspiration to write this book.

All my survey responders, including Mills, Delilah, Sophie, Elise, Holly, Lexi, Kathy, Killian, Bailey, Kitty, Grace and Grub.

Dr Judy Green our GP, for her sage advice and willingness to be collared!

Professor Andrea Cavanna, for diagnosing our son's Tourette's Syndrome and for supporting his educational needs assessment that allowed him to reach his potential.

Jane-Anne Bird, formerly SENCo, for listening, responding and providing our primary point of contact in school.

Christopher John Payne, for providing me with the structure to write the book and offering clarity and constructive criticism throughout its development.

Caroline Carr, my writing 'buddy', for reading through multiple drafts and moral support throughout.

Debbie Emmitt, my Editor, for her friendly professionalism, for pointing out all my style inconsistencies and ensuring that the book was readable.

Rebekah Grace Kienzle, my Illustrator, for her brilliant interpretation of my stick figure ideas, her willingness to make endless tweaks to rough sketches to arrive at the final result, and her enthusiasm for the whole project.

Simon Hough, my Designer and Formatter, for his infinite patience in turning my scrappy manuscript into a book I could be proud of.

Ken Leeder, my Cover Designer, for making sure that first impressions count.

Foreword

I first met Dr Mandy Barnett when her son was referred to me for diagnosis and management of Tourette's Syndrome. He clearly fitted the criteria, although he was only mildly affected. During one of his consultations, she explained how her son was struggling with his writing, especially in tests at school. I had written a paper on 'over-writing' which I was able to forward on to his school and this enabled him to access more support, fortunately early enough to allow him to obtain the GCSE results that he deserved.

With her background in psychology, medicine and medical education, as well as being a parent, Mandy Barnett understands the importance of supporting children and teenagers both at home and in school.

Tourette's Syndrome is a complex disorder, best known for its more extreme versions. I am well aware that there are many young people in the community whom I never get to see as a specialist. Milder forms often go undiagnosed and unsupported, and this can impact hugely on emotional wellbeing and learning development.

This book addresses that gap admirably. It is written primarily for parents but is also a valuable guide for teachers and for students trying to explain their condition to adults and access the support they need. It is medically accurate but easy to read, and includes lots of practical details and tips from someone with first-hand experience. If you are a parent, carer or teacher with a child in their care who makes inexplicable noises or movements or whose behaviour you don't understand but who appears to be struggling either at home or in the classroom, I highly recommend that you read it.

Last but not least, Dr Barnett's book highlights the importance of building on the person's strengths, above and beyond – often alongside – the presence of their tics. This is an all too neglected message that deserves to be shared because of its life-changing potential.

Professor Andrea E Cavanna

Professor of neuropsychiatry and consultant in behavioural neurology at the Department of Neuropsychiatry, Birmingham and Solihull Mental Health NHS Foundation Trust, UK.

Introduction

TOURETTE'S SYNDROME is much more common than most people realise, and since the Covid-19 pandemic and national lockdowns around the world more and more cases are emerging.

However, it is all too easy to miss early signs or mild cases, as well as to make the wrong diagnosis.

My own children (a now young adult son, and a daughter in her mid-teens) were diagnosed after I had spotted the early signs, found out about Tourette's (abbreviated to TS) and then asked for help. As a doctor I was trained to spot 'signs', and I knew where to look and how to 'work the system', yet it still wasn't easy.

Since my children were diagnosed and the more I have investigated it, the more I realised that:

- To be directed to reading the right books, there is an expectation that you already know that your child has Tourette's.
- Films and TV documentaries focus on the more severe manifestations and associated problems affecting kids with TS. This makes for engaging viewing, but may intimidate the 'new' TS parent or cause them to think their child does not have the condition at all.
- Many of the 'memoir' style of books are written from a US perspective with an emphasis on private medical care and

medication, yet most kids with TS have minimal contact with medical experts.

- The books written by experts in the field cover all the possible associated disorders. This is important and inclusive, but for a parent just starting to get to grips with TS, it can make the whole area feel like a minefield.

Therefore, I decided to write this book for you, the parent or carer who is just considering that their child may have TS and wants to know the next steps. It may also be useful for the young person involved, as they can use it to convince you and their teachers that they are not making it up or mucking about. This is both infuriating and deeply distressing for the young person and became the driver for me to get this book finished!

My 'seven Cs' approach combines research-based evidence and theory with anecdotes from my own children and family, and quotes from teens in a Discord group (self-administered online community) to which my daughter belongs. Their views are especially relevant, as a number of them have experienced newly emerging or changes in their tics during the pandemic.

As I am based in the UK, I am going to focus on how to work with our own NHS and state education systems, with all their flaws and imperfections. To get the best possible outcomes for your child, you need to choose your battles wisely. If you live elsewhere in the world, the principles remain the same, but your systems may be different.

As a post-pandemic parent (I will use this term throughout the book but please take it to apply to any 'carer' relationship) you may be feeling stretched; you may have lost your job or be dealing with economic uncertainty; you may have suffered a relationship breakdown; you may have lost loved ones or have been ill yourself; you may have more than one child to cope with and have been trying to home-school.

This book is not about trying to load you with more challenges or guilt at not meeting all your child's needs. It is about giving you clarity and a simple toolkit of things you can do (or not do) to make life easier.

Good luck!

Mandy Barnett

Disclaimer: Although I am a qualified doctor and clinical educator, trained in psychology and communication skills, I am not a specialist in neurodevelopmental disorders, nor a children's teacher or therapist. This book is aimed at pointing you towards those who are.

About the Author

Dr Mandy M Barnett
Photo of author by Angelica James

Dr Mandy M Barnett is a psychology graduate, clinical educator and retired consultant physician who worked for over 30 years in the NHS, and as an Associate Clinical Professor at Warwick Medical School (WMS).

She has a master's degree in clinical education and a doctorate in communication skills. As a specialist in End-of-Life care, she worked with healthcare teams, patients and their families to optimize communication and quality of life. As an educator, she designed and taught courses in medicine and communication skills to medical students, doctors, nurses and other healthcare professionals. She also ran the final written examinations and represented WMS at the Universities Medical Assessment Partnership. As a Fellow of the Royal College of Physicians she helped design questions for final specialty examinations.

She has two children, Alex and Angelica, who both have Tourette's Syndrome. She lives with them, her husband Patrick and their dog Lola in Warwickshire in the UK.

The Seven Cs Approach

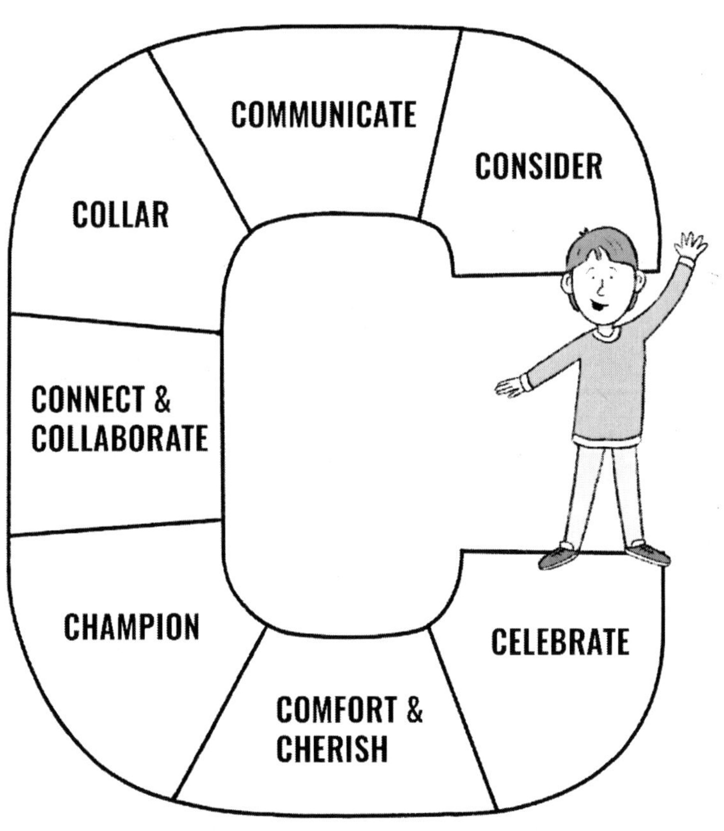

CHAPTER 1

Consider the Possibility

Could my child have Tourette's?

CHAPTER 1

Consider the Possibility

Could my child have Tourette's?

First things first – what is it? FAQs about Tourette's

Tourette's Syndrome (TS) is defined in medical journals as a neurodevelopmental disorder[1] (i.e. a condition of the nervous system and brain, not a mental illness). It was first described in 1885 by Georges Gilles de la Tourette. For many years it was thought to have either an anatomical basis (something wrong with the shape of the brain) or at the other extreme to be rooted in psychological conflict (a viewpoint heavily influenced by the theories of Sigmund Freud), with the psychological theory persisting until as recently as the 1960s.

In the late 1960s the American husband-and-wife team Drs Arthur and Elaine Shapiro showed that medical drug treatment could be effective in dampening down tics. They worked alongside a New York parent group who founded the Tourette Syndrome Association in the US in 1972 and succeeded in getting Tourette's reclassified from a psychological to a neurological disorder.

In more recent years, since its modern reclassification as a neurodevelopmental disorder, it is now seen as a 'symptom syndrome' rather than a disease.

Further advances have been made in the last 30 years with the development of sophisticated brain-imaging techniques like dynamic MRI (magnetic resonance imaging), which allows scientists to study in real time the brains of living people with Tourette's, as they think and tic. TS is now thought to be due to a malfunction in the neural circuits between the basal ganglia and other areas in the brain – a form of 'short-circuiting'[2].

What exactly are tics?

Tics can be any sudden twitch, movement or sound that a person does repeatedly and involuntarily. They can be simple, such as blinking one eye or sniffing, or complex, such as throwing an object or speaking a complete phrase. Tics usually occur in bouts, with intervals in between. In Tourette's the tics tend to become more complex and more frequent as the child gets older.

How common is it?

Full-blown Tourette's Syndrome represents one end of a spectrum of tic disorders, but it is more common than previously recognised. One reason it used to be considered rare was that it was largely hidden or ignored, except for people who were severely affected. However, if all the mild cases are taken into account, the numbers go up.

It is now thought that at least 1 in 100 children could have TS. This means that in an average secondary school year group of 200 kids, there are at least two with TS. In an average-sized primary school of 300 kids, there will be at least three showing early signs. In a recent study of schoolchildren in Spain, the number was even higher with 5% (1 in 20) meeting the criteria[3].

Is it genetic?

Yes, but not as obviously as it may seem. Tourette's is inherited in a complex way, through both genetic and environmental causes[4]. It is thought to be passed through several genes, and that any child of someone with Tourette's has a 25%–50% chance of inheriting it. It therefore runs in families, but because it may present in very mild forms and can disappear altogether, previous generations may well not have recognised it.

If you think about it, if children today can (and do) get to late teens or early adulthood before their TS is diagnosed, what chance did kids stand 30 or more years ago?

However, if you can go back and ask your partner or family members, you are likely to discover that it was present in previous generations.

> *My husband vaguely remembers having some tics as a child but grew out of them during his teens. His father has signs of obsessive-compulsive disorder as did his great-uncle.*

It is more commonly expressed in boys than girls by about 4:1, and it also appears more commonly in White vs Afro-Caribbean or Asian populations, but the reasons for this are yet unknown. It is not clear if the apparent racial and ethnic group differences are real or represent under-diagnosis[5]. In a 2017 US film documentary, it was suggested that subtle tics could have been mis-diagnosed as attention deficit hyperactivity disorder (ADHD), especially in Black boys[6].

Can you catch it?

Tourette's is not an infectious disease, so if you don't have the genes for it, you won't develop it. However, what causes some people with the genes to develop the condition and others not is unclear. In addition, kids with tics can set off tics in other kids; this is something I will discuss further in later chapters.

Is it progressive?

The answer is no but...

Unlike conditions such as Parkinson's Disease that cause permanent worsening physical changes affecting the underlying nerve cells and pathways, Tourette's Syndrome does not progress in the same way.

In TS, the underlying nervous system and brain are healthy, and it **does not shorten life expectancy**.

However, whilst in the majority of affected children, tics will subside in late teens and early adulthood, in about one third they can increase in severity and in a small number this can significantly affect their ability to function in adulthood, so in that sense, it can 'progress'.

Is it curable?

There isn't a simple answer to this, although it's one of the first questions you might want to ask. Because Tourette's develops so differently in individuals over time, it can disappear without a diagnosis ever being made; in other words it 'cures' itself. However, the underlying differences in the brains of people with Tourette's cannot be cured by any single or simple treatment, although their tics and symptoms can be managed in a variety of ways. In that sense it is incurable.

It's not all about swearing! Types of tics in Tourette's

The popular perception of Tourette's is that of someone swearing loudly – the official medical term for this is **coprolalia.** In reality, this represents under 10% of the vocal tics experienced so is pretty uncommon.

However, because tics in TS emerge, evolve and disappear, vocal tics involving swear words can also come and go. It can be very distressing to the person to open their mouth and hear language emerge that they wouldn't dream of using consciously. It can also be problematic as swearing tics may be uttered loudly in inappropriate settings such as in the street. Particularly for teenage boys, it may be interpreted as a provocation either by other teens or by authority figures such as the police.

> *My daughter Angelica doesn't swear voluntarily, but sometimes she has a 'sweary' tic. She can feel it building up and if she doesn't want to feel or cause embarrassment, she will disguise it by 'coughing' – during the COVID-19 pandemic this had its own problems!*

The movement-tic equivalent of coprolalia is **copropraxia**. This refers to a situation where the young person makes obscene gestures such as 'the middle finger'. It rarely occurs without coprolalia and is much less common[7]. Interestingly, it has been observed that in the uncommon but recognised cases of young people with deafness alongside their Tourette's who communicate via sign language rather than speech, they may sign tic obscenities[8].

Non-obscene socially inappropriate symptoms (NOSIS)

Another associated problem can be racist or homophobic phrases. The child comes out with the very words that they are most trying not to think or say, and the more anxious they become, the more likely they are to tic. Because the words themselves sound organised, it is easy for them to be mistaken as deliberate, or in the case of young children, to be taken as reflecting the views of the adult with them.

A similar problem can be observed in situations such as airports or other 'security conscious' settings. We have all experienced the desire to say something stupid when asked questions like 'Did you pack your luggage yourself' or on immigration forms 'Are you a terrorist'?

For the person with Tourette's, this can be a tic nightmare. A recent UK television documentary about a family with two young sons with TS illustrated this perfectly[9]. Having made the brave decision to travel abroad for the first time, the mum very sensibly contacted the authorities at Eurostar in advance to explain her children's condition, and to emphasise that if one of them inadvertently ticced under stress and shouted, 'I've got a bomb,' this was not the case. Fortunately, they were allowed to board with minimal waiting, and all went well.

An interesting observation in the same documentary was that, contrary to their fears about going to a theme park in Germany with two ticcing youngsters trying not to shout 'Nazi' or 'Hitler', all went well[9]. In the context of a lot of excited children, children shouting random words in English passed all but unnoticed. I shall discuss social outings further in Chapter 6.

As well as verbal NOSIS, the young person may develop movement tics that are also socially inappropriate, such as patting an older family member or a stranger on the head, or more disturbingly, on the bottom. It is easy to see how this can be misinterpreted.

Echolalia and echopraxia

Echolalia is a form of vocal tic in which the child repeats a word or phrase that they have heard someone else say. This may be done repetitively or just as a single utterance.

It may be said in the child's 'own' tic voice or may take the form of an exact mimic, sometimes with an uncanny level of accuracy.

Teens with TS are particularly susceptible to this feature. This may be in part due to the rise of chatrooms, streaming, memes etc on the internet, sat nav in cars and artificial intelligence (AI) like Alexa and Siri at home.

Sometimes echolalia can be immediate i.e. a direct response to what has just been said. Other times it can be delayed.

> *Angelica often tics quotable lines from films or TV shows that she has enjoyed:*
>
> *'I've been falling for 30 minutes!' (quoting Loki from the Marvel film Thor: Ragnarok)*
>
> *'Wow, it's like a bloomin' spaceship.' (quoting Pat from the BBC TV comedy series Ghosts)*

An interesting crossover between echolalia and coprolalia can sometimes be heard amongst teens whose native language is not English, but who follow English-speaking streamers with Tourette's (see Chapter 7 for further discussion). Whilst they will usually tic in their first language, if they have coprolalia this may include swear words both in their own language and in English, e.g. a French teen may tic 'Merde' (sh*t) or 'F*ck'.

The movement-tic equivalent of echolalia is **echopraxia**, in which the person repeats a movement or action that they have observed (usually in real time). It may appear co-ordinated (such as picking up a phone) but occurs involuntarily and is uncomfortable to resist. Think of when you see someone yawning!

Palilalia and palipraxia

These are similar in nature to echolalia and echopraxia, but in this form of tic the person repeats their own sound or action, rather than mirroring someone else's. Unlike a stutter, it usually occurs at the end of a phrase or sentence and typically the person will repeat complete words or phrases, e.g. 'That's great, thank you thank you thank you'.

This type of tic can be very subtle and easy to miss. It is common for young children to repeat words or phrases as part of their normal language development. Verbal and movement repetition can also be a feature of autism spectrum disorder (ASD), so distinguishing between them in the early stages may not be straightforward.

Mental tics

These are 'internal' verbal tics that people with Tourette's frequently experience but don't usually mention unless asked. They tend to be words or short phrases that the person 'hears' in their head, but unlike the conscious inner 'voice' that many people use when thinking or planning an action, a mental tic is random and not usually connected to what the person is thinking about.

Although these mental tics do not necessarily have negative or anxiety-provoking components and therefore do not always cause disruption to the person's conscious mood, they can impede concentration.

Some examples of Angelica's mental tics are: 'lemon' or 'Yes, he'd make a very fine soldier' (quoting Captain, again from the BBC TV comedy series Ghosts)

All Touretters have tics, but not all ticcers have Tourette's – a simple three-point checklist

For a child or teen to be diagnosed with Tourette's Syndrome, they must tick (no pun intended) every item on the following three-point checklist:

1. **At least one vocal tic**
2. **Motor tics (movement-based or involving muscles)**
3. **Present for at least a year – but must also change**

A child with a single stable facial twitch does not have Tourette's. However, a child with Tourette's can display both slowly evolving or rapidly changing tics. Tics can also be under-diagnosed – a child who sniffs or clears their throat repetitively has a vocal tic; motor tics can also be very subtle, or mistaken for clumsiness, such as a child who appears to trip over their own feet.

My son Alex's first tic was a repetitive blinking of his right eye. When we asked him what the problem was, he told us it felt 'irritated' – he even received treatment for conjunctivitis. It was only when it failed to resolve, and he was able to explain that the 'irritation' was more a sense of a need to blink rather than eye soreness, that we began to understand.

However, it took several more months before he developed further tics – first a squeaking noise, and then more worryingly a motor tic that involved him flinging his arm out, causing actual pain in his elbow. Then the penny dropped.

The fluidity of tics in TS is a key feature; this can mean a motor tic being replaced by a verbal tic, or both present together, or tics changing every few months, weeks or even days.

Angelica has what she calls 'scattering' days when her verbal tics evolve back and forth 'looking' for something to settle on – sometimes a word or phrase that had disappeared will re-emerge; other times a new noise or phrase will appear.

Think of it like the UK weather in spring, which can go from sunshine to snow in a matter of hours!

CURIOUSER AND CURIOUSER!

Similarity to other conditions

Some features of TS are shared with other conditions. It is not uncommon for kids with TS to have features of attention deficit hyperactivity disorder (ADHD), or of obsessive-compulsive disorder (OCD).

Attention deficit hyperactivity disorder (ADHD)

ADHD is a well-recognised disorder, but it is a lesser-known fact that ADHD is commonly associated with TS (over 50% of people who have one condition, have both) and that ADHD may appear in pre-schoolers before any TS tics emerge.

Obsessive-compulsive disorder (OCD)

This is another well-known condition, but it is less recognised that it can be associated with Tourette's Syndrome, or indeed may be the only disorder demonstrated by someone carrying the genes for Tourette's, as we observed in our own family.

Again, many people are familiar with some of the most well-known OCD examples such as compulsive handwashing, but almost any repeatable behaviour can form the basis of a compulsion, e.g. tapping the ground with your foot, stroking a smooth door handle. For children with Tourette's, it has been noted that the most common compulsions are usually less to do with cleanliness and more often the need to create a visual or tactile sense of order or symmetry[6] (see Chapter 3 for further discussion).

Children can also suffer from 'intrusive thoughts' which are usually (although not exclusively) unpleasant or anxiety-provoking.

> *Alex used to get very distressed (from about age five onwards) about what he called 'scary thoughts'. Looking back, these may have been 'intrusive thoughts'.*

Both conditions can cause problems for the child at school, which I shall discuss further in Chapter 4.

RAGE (repeated anger generated episodes) attacks

This is a common feature of Tourette's Syndrome and may appear before or alongside tics. If RAGE attacks come first, it is extremely easy to misunderstand them, which can be very distressing for both child and carers. They usually (although not exclusively) occur when the child is stressed or tired.

> *Alex never had the typical 'terrible twos' tantrums, which made his later episodes of rage during primary school all the more upsetting and difficult to understand. He was generally mild-tempered and empathic but would 'fly off the handle' for no reason, usually when tired at the end of a school day. Afterwards, he would be terribly upset because he couldn't explain why he had got angry. It was only after he was diagnosed with TS that we could look back and realise he had been having 'RAGE attacks'.*

Autism spectrum disorder (ASD)

In recent years there has been interest and research into possible genetic links between ASD and Tourette's, and there do appear to be higher rates of ASD among children diagnosed with Tourette's compared with the general population. However, it is not clear if this is a definite link or whether some of the measures used to diagnose ASD, namely the presence of repetitive behaviours, are simply picking up children with TS combined with obsessive-compulsive disorder. At present this remains an area of exploration rather than offering definitive answers[10].

Other associated problems and disorders

- Anxiety
- Depression
- Sleep problems
- Sensory defensiveness (heightened negative reaction to sounds, smells or tactile sensations)
- Fine motor skills problems (control of movement such as writing) (see Chapter 4 for further discussion)
- Executive dysfunction (difficulties with problem-solving and organising action)
- Social skills problems

The list is a lengthy one, and it is beyond the scope of this book to discuss them all, but that does not mean that your child will have all or even any of them. However, if you are aware of the possibilities, they may explain things that you have observed but not understood, and it may be especially important when it comes to supporting your child.

Chapter 1: Parent Action Points	
1	Tourette's is common – your child could have it. Consider it possible and do not dismiss it.
2	Pay attention to your child's 'habits' – they could be tics or associated conditions. Start noting any patterns or changes and ask them if they can tell you how they feel.
3	You can't prevent your child having TS, but you can start to gather evidence to take to experts – this could be invaluable. Note when the first 'habit' appeared and when new ones develop, especially if some involve sound and others movement.
4	Ask your nearest and dearest (if they're genetically related to your child) if they remember having any twitches or habits themselves, or any older relatives who had them.
5	Don't panic – in most cases, Tourette's is mild in its effects and often disappears entirely by the time your child reaches adulthood.

CHAPTER 2

Communicate with Your Child and Family

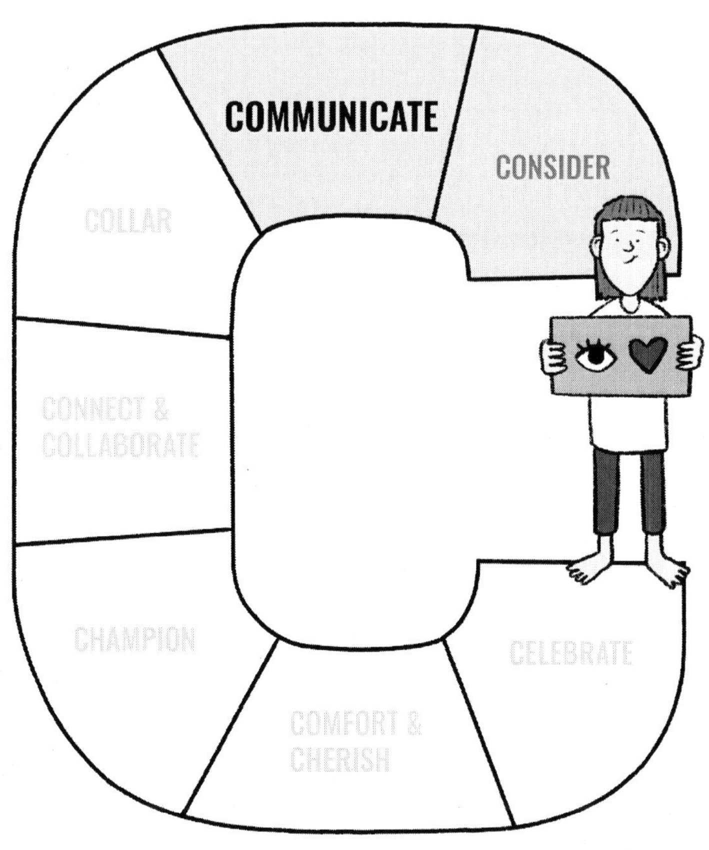

CHAPTER 2

Communicate with Your Child and Family

Teenage survey

As part of my research for writing this book, I wrote a short survey for the teenagers on a Discord server, known as the Uncontrollables. This is an online support network for people with tics or Tourette's to which my daughter belongs.

At the time I sent them the survey, the group had approximately 100 members, of whom 14 completed it.

I have incorporated some of their experiences throughout this book, including direct quotes where they have given me permission to do so.

This is not a 'scientific' study, in that respondents were self-selecting as members of the group and were free to answer whether or not they had a formal diagnosis of TS. However, their responses clearly illustrate some of the difficulties that young Touretters face, and what sort of help and support they appreciate.

Tourette's can emerge at any point from about the age of five into the mid-teens. Most commonly the early tics are behaviours like blinking, sniffing, throat clearing or grunting, all of which can easily be dismissed as 'habits'.

When I asked my survey group at what age they remembered having their first tic, six out of 14 said between the ages of 5 and 12.

In one case it was:

"as far as I can remember" (Delilah, 14, US)

Younger children with TS can struggle to explain the problem, but equally, they are less likely to feel embarrassed or inhibited; this is something they learn over time from the reactions of people around them.

As the child gets older, they can often start to describe what they feel like when they tic – the so-called 'premonitory urge':

> *Angelica describes her 'premonitory urge' as a physical sense of 'irritation', for which the nearest equivalent she can find is the need to yawn.*

How you respond as a parent or family member is critical and can be enormously helpful or detrimental in equal measure.

Ticcing at home – the importance of acknowledgement and acceptance

As a parent, it is important that you open up communication with your child and with the rest of your family members about what is going on. Your child or teen may be feeling upset, confused, scared and embarrassed. Siblings may find their behaviour difficult to understand and annoying or even frightening.

Encourage your child, if they are old enough, to describe how they feel when they are ticcing and reassure them that you know they can't help doing it. They may already have some sense of what makes it worse or better and you can then work with them.

If you acknowledge your child's tics and offer that crucial safe space, your youngster can relax at home. You are also opening channels for them to raise issues as these emerge in other settings such as school.

Family relationships – denial and guilt

If the genetic component has come from your own family, you may remember similar behaviours that were not talked about or were frowned upon. Likewise, if it was your partner or their family who were affected, they may be in denial that there is a problem. This could be either because they 'grew out of it' or because they feel a sense of shame or guilt that they have 'passed it on', especially if they have negative memories of their own childhood. Traditional fathers in particular may struggle with not being able to 'fix the problem' and may withdraw, leaving the mum to deal both with their own feelings and those of the child (apologies for sweeping generalisations; I am paraphrasing the comments of some of the fathers themselves)[1].

It is important to recognise that **no one is to blame, to acknowledge mixed emotions and, in a two-parent household, to discuss and agree how to approach any problems together** (although this may be more easily said than done).

In our own family situation, as a doctor, I was the obvious parent to research what was happening to our son and to offer him support, but I think that my husband was more than happy to let me get on with it!

Tics can take off

It is often at home that the greatest variety of tics emerge.

A key feature of Tourette's is both the range and fluidity of tics. Quotes from my survey group illustrate how many kinds of tics there are and how wide-ranging they can be for any single individual:

"Motors: arm jerk, 'calling' phone hand gesture, the Spider-Man hand gesture, the middle finger (unfortunately), blinking, winking, jaw locking, scrunching nose, banging collar bone. My vocal tics tend to vary a lot as in they frequently change. Right now I have, 'Ahh pigeon,' 'It's me, Mario,' 'Brrah' (like a weird noise), whistling and I repeat my own and other people's words." (Mills, 16, UK)

"Head jerks, popping my mouth, straightening the hand, middle finger, whistling, hitting walls, saying 'wow' and 'hey', squeaking, breathing tics (only at nights), back flexing, the 'beans' one, echolalia, rolling my eyes to the right side, blinking, throwing things and some others." (Sophie, Poland)

"Wow, way too many. Vocal: beans, wow, get out, gasping and 'cuckoo'; motor: neck jerk, lip-smacking, twirling head in figure eights that can last for up to 30 seconds (makes me really dizzy), hitting walls, hitting my chest and head, eye blinking, my knees will lock and I can't walk, etc. there are so many more!" (Lexi, 14, US)

Angelica describes 'scatter' days as when old vocal tics fade away and her tic 'alter ego' appears to be looking for new words or phrases to hang on to; usually things that she sees. This can be tiring: "It's like my brain is constantly on the lookout for something to tic about."

These vocalisations are often short-lived, although alongside them are more consistent 'chirrups'. After a day or so, new vocal tics will emerge and settle for a while. She has noticed that 'scatter days' increase when she has been stressed for long periods (such as during GCSE mock exams).

Hiding away

If youngsters do not feel able to tic freely at home, they will often retreat to a private space:

"My room is good for not letting sound out if there is a towel or blanket by the door, so I do that to keep my vocals that I can't suppress quiet and then I keep myself occupied so I'm focussed and tic less." (Mills, 16, UK)

"I do my best to suppress my tics around my family and have tic attacks in my bed." (Elise, 13, US)

The most important thing I can stress is that, no matter how 'organised' the tic appears to be, it **really is involuntary**, i.e. the child cannot help doing it.

Angelica describes the feeling of experiencing one of her motor tics as being 'like a puppet' – she knows her arm is moving but she does not feel any sense of control. Yet to an outside observer, she is 'intentionally' throwing a pencil off her desk.

The single most supportive thing you can do for your child is to **believe them**.

Not faking it

Unfortunately, a significant number of youngsters find that their families dismiss their tics either as attention-seeking or even suggest that they are 'faking it'.

> *One of Angelica's school friends has several vocal tics, although she remains undiagnosed. Her mother has noticed but tells her to 'stop making fun of people with Tourette's!'*

In responses to my survey, the idea that tics could represent attention-seeking was mentioned more than once in reference to the home environment:

"Most of the time I suppress around my guardians...when I do tic, they just brush it off or say I'm doing it for attention." (Mills, 16, UK)

"They think I'm faking." (Delilah, 14, US)

Not only are they not 'faking it', but there is documented evidence that people with a known diagnosis of TS tic more when they are alone, i.e. when there is no 'benefit' as they are unobserved[2].

Indeed, some tics can be so severe that they cause involuntary self-harm.

> *One of Angelica's current tics involves hitting the side of her hand on the table or arm of her chair when she is trying to*

study, with enough frequency and force as to cause bruising.

Similar problems were reported by some of the survey responders:

"I struggle to read, I hurt my hand, I stutter, I am anxious of people, I'm always tired, I've got tic attacks." (Sophie, Poland)

"Tics can sometimes come in forms of self-harm like hitting yourself. Just last month I had a tic attack and scratched my face up really bad, the tic continued after the attack, and I had to put a gigantic Band-Aid over it to keep me from reopening it :(that's just one example of how it sucks." (Lexi, 14, US)

Being teased

In other situations, some may experience teasing from family members. Sometimes this happens because the family do not recognise the tics as Tourette's, but it may still occur even when the family appreciate the involuntary nature of the tics.

One teen reported that, although her family recognised her TS insofar as she was now being taken to the doctor for a diagnosis, they still:

> ***"ridicule me to the point where I have to suppress". (Delilah, 14, US)***

Another teen reports her family:

> ***"laugh at some of my tics and say some of my trigger words". (Elise, 13, US)***

This was true even in our own family:

> *When Alex first developed vocal tics, they were a mixture of squeaks and 'whoops'. Dad thought this was amusing and would sometimes 'whoop' back, causing our son to 'whoop' again. His younger sister would also copy as she saw her dad doing it, to our son's intense irritation.*

If the overall home environment is positive and accepting, your child may be able to take the teasing in good part, but check this with them, especially if they have tics that are painful.

Beyond the immediate family, it may be helpful to explain to other family members and friends (if your child is older, ask for their permission first) that what they hear or see are 'tic' behaviours and not the child being rude or naughty.

"People say that I'm not paying attention and being rude because when I roll my eyes, I look like I'm not listening to them." (Sophie, Poland)

This is especially important if the tics are loud or involve swear words or obscene gestures. It will head off well-meaning but critical responses aimed either directly at the child or at your own parenting skills.

Talking to the family may also lead indirectly to relatives volunteering information about previous generations that supports the current diagnosis.

Parenting a child or teen with coprolalia

Although only a small percentage of children with Tourette's develop persistent coprolalia, swearing tics will come and go. When a child exhibits coprolalia, it is important to learn the difference between conscious swearing and ticcing.

In conscious swearing, the child will use a variety of expletives and will usually express them either as a descriptive part of a phrase, e.g. 'I'm having a cr*p day', or 'I hate my f*cking school' or as a standalone expression of emotion such as surprise or anger ('Oh f*ck', 'Sh*t'), usually spoken in the tone associated with that emotion.

In contrast, tics that are swear words or phrases containing swear words come out randomly, either during a completely unrelated sentence or conversation, or as a single expression. Crucially, they are not associated with the person's mood or emotion at the time.

It is also usually said (or shouted) consistently in the same tone and pitch, which may differ from the person's normal speaking voice, e.g. 'I'm going to the shops – **F*ck off** – do you want me to get you anything?'

Some while ago, I observed an amusing moment in a TV news report about young adults with Tourette's in which a 20-something young woman was being interviewed at home with her mum in the background. She ticced 'f*ck' and other expletives numerous times, but it was only when she said that something 'f*cking annoyed' her that her mum chipped in and told her to stop swearing!

Is it Tourette's or just tics? Does it make a difference?

Going back to my point in Chapter 1 – all Touretters have tics, but not all ticcers have Tourette's. However, from your child's viewpoint, it does not matter which they are. As reported in the medical press and through research studies, a great many youngsters started ticcing during the pandemic.

The numbers reaching the attention of specialist referral centres have gone up exponentially, but this is the tip of the iceberg. We know that the process for referral is slow in the UK. In addition, either many children with tics have not raised the problem or their families have not recognised it. So, the actual numbers are likely to be much higher than those officially reported. In my survey group, whilst 13 out of 14 believed they had TS, only four had received an official diagnosis; another reported her neurologist was waiting for a year to elapse (diagnostically correct), whilst another said that she had to wait until she was 18 (not a medical requirement for diagnosis but may reflect access to adult services only).

Some of these youngsters will have previously undiagnosed

TS, others will have a functional tic disorder related to anxiety provoked by the pandemic and exams – my 14th respondent believed that was the case for her:

"I blame school mocks." (Grub, 16, UK)

However, what matters to the child is that you as their parent or carer recognise that they are not ticcing for fun or attention.

RAGE (repeated anger generated episodes) attacks

As a parent, you are likely to be the person to notice emerging tics or RAGE attacks first because both can be subtle and easily mistaken for voluntary movement or tantrums. They also tend to get worse when the child is tired, such as at the end of a school day.

> *I remember feeling terribly upset when Alex started to have 'RAGE attacks' from about the age of five. I would dread picking him up from school. Ironically, I made it worse by sending him to after-school club even on days when I could have collected him earlier because I felt I could not cope with him, so he would be more tired and even more inclined to have a 'tantrum' when he got home. Once he got his diagnosis and I understood that it was a feature of his Tourette's, I felt less of a failure as a parent, and he felt relieved that he was not being 'bad'.*

Other behavioural issues

Children with Tourette's can behave inappropriately or unpredictably in several ways:

- Crying
- Over-reacting
- Throwing things
- Impulsive behaviour

These can all be easily misinterpreted as 'naughtiness' or 'being difficult'.

> *We were outside our new house talking to a neighbour with children of similar ages to ours, whilst the children rode their bicycles and scooters around the green in front of the houses. To our horror, Alex (then aged eight) suddenly threw his scooter into the path of one of the other children, causing her to fall off her bike. When we asked him why he had done it, he had no idea.*

It is important to differentiate such behavioural issues from the child's normal personality. Kids with TS are not anti-social, although they may become withdrawn and shy if they are not supported at home.

Being enabled to let their tics or other behaviours 'out' in a safe environment is key to helping them accept their TS as a part of who they are, without their diagnosis becoming their defining feature.

However, it can be equally distressing if their tics are noticed but ignored or not acknowledged by their family:

"They think that they are just tics related to anxiety, not anything else, despite a tic-disorder diagnosis. They also want to 'fix' me and believe that the tics will just disappear." (Grace, 17, UK)

> ***"They think it's just something I do when I'm nervous because they don't notice the more violent ones." (Kitty, 16, UK)***

Another said simply she would like her family to:

> ***"acknowledge their existence." (Elise, 13, US).***

As several respondents to my survey pointed out, tics are not fun; they are not quirky; they are exhausting and "*really, really hard*".

This is especially the case when a tic involves repetitive movement that could cause harm or breakages, e.g. throwing a cup of hot coffee, or vocal tics such as throat clearing that becomes uncomfortable.

In my survey, eight out of 14 respondents reported being able to tic freely at home, but six did not.

If they are not supported at home, they can end up feeling deeply isolated. This came across strongly in the survey responses, when asked what they would like their family to do differently:

> ***"Let me be me." (Delilah, 14, US)***

> ***"Listen to me." (Mills, 16, UK)***

> ***"I would like them [parents] to know I can't control my tics and provide a little bit of comfort when I do tic around them." (Elise, 13, US)***

IT ISN'T MY FAULT!

Dr B Duncan McKinlay (aka 'Dr Dunc'), a Canadian psychologist, has made it his life's work to educate others about Tourette's. He had tics from early childhood but no one in his family or school community recognised the problem. He finally self-diagnosed late in his high school years when he read a description of Tourette's in the 'Ann Landers' (agony aunt) advice column.

In his documentary 'Life's a Twitch'[3], Dr Dunc describes quite poignantly his sense of being a freak in his small town, acutely aware of his otherness but not understanding what the problem was. Unfortunately he was also unsupported by his parents. His self-esteem was so low that on several occasions during his childhood and teens he attempted suicide.

One of the saddest responses I received in my survey was from the teen who felt more able to tic at school than at home:

"I hide in my room and suppress until school." (Killian, 14, Canada)

In contrast, if you acknowledge their TS, it can make an enormous difference. One of my respondents described how her family recognised her TS, even though they were still waiting for the one-year duration mark for her to receive a formal diagnosis, and what this meant to her:

"They're there to support me and help however they can."

This in turn:

"makes me feel heard and believed; it helps me have hope." (Lexi, 13, US)

Chapter 2: Parent Action Points	
1	Believe your child.
2	Don't tell them to stop.
3	Don't suggest they are faking it.
4	Don't tease them about their tics.
5	Allow them to feel comfortable ticcing at home – but don't pretend it's not happening.
6	Talk about the tics with your child and the rest of the family; reassure your child that they are not 'mad' or 'bad'.

CHAPTER 3

Collar Your GP!

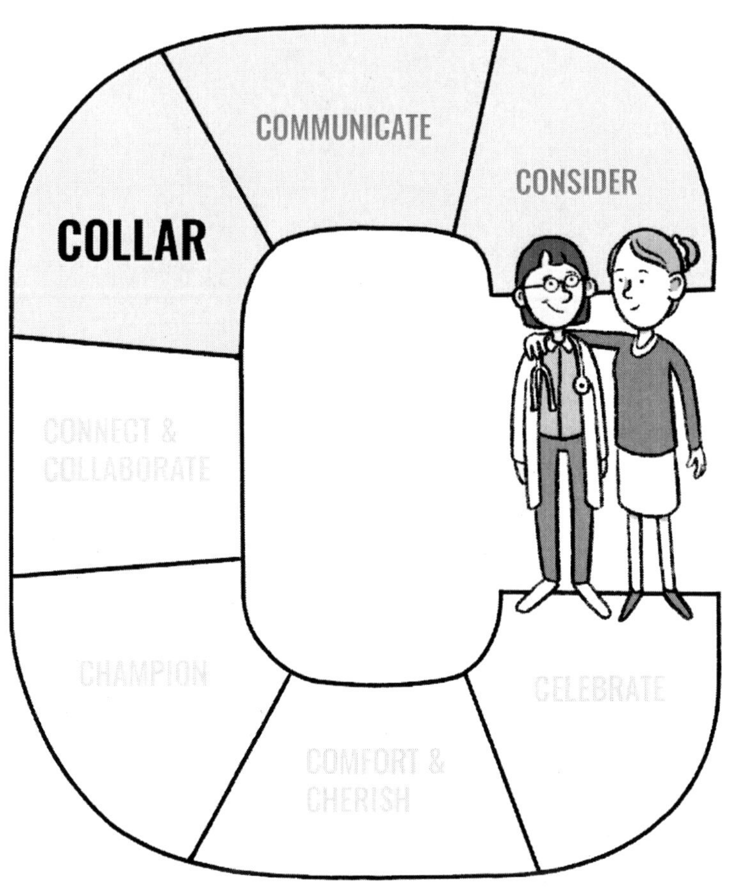

CHAPTER 3

Collar Your GP!

Even (or especially) if you do not know what is going on, it is important to make an appointment with your general practitioner (GP) (or family practitioner in the US) early in your child's journey with Tourette's.

This is not always easy (and especially difficult following the COVID-19 pandemic), but GPs are still open for normal business. Although many GPs limit their face-to-face appointments, many practices now offer telephone and remote video consultations, and these can work perfectly well for an initial discussion.

In the UK and across many European countries, the path to further help depends on getting a clear diagnosis. Tourette's is a neurodevelopmental disorder, not an illness, but accessing the right support does require a 'label'. Paradoxically, this is all the more important if your child appears to be only mildly affected, as more subtle disabilities can easily be missed or dismissed.

> *When I first took our son, Alex, to our GP, she acknowledged that his 'presenting features' fitted Tourette's, but she asked me if I really wanted him referred to a specialist service – to 'medicalise' what appeared to be a very mild form of the condition. The short answer to this was 'Yes'.*

COLLAR YOUR GP

There are three important points to remember here:

- Referral to specialist neurodevelopmental services in the UK can take an exceedingly long time. It is not uncommon to wait more than a year just for an assessment.
- Whilst the initial presentation may be mild, a characteristic of Tourette's is that tics come and go. In two out of three cases they will eventually subside to an un-noticeable or manageable level, but in one in three cases they will persist into adulthood and may cause significant disability. Because many tics do subside and it is the adult group that need ongoing help and support, one of the problems in getting a diagnosis in children is that there are fewer specialists in

TS (in the UK at least) available to see under-16s.

- Due to the age at which Tourette's generally presents, and as a direct result of long waiting times and lack of child specialists, your child may be well into secondary (high) school before they receive their 'label'.

There are also several associated conditions that can sometimes blur the picture.

Attention deficit hyperactivity disorder (ADHD)

ADHD is well known and recognised and tends to run in families. Children with ADHD usually have symptoms of inattentiveness, fidgety behaviour, short attention span and impulsiveness, i.e. acting without thinking. It can also be associated with Tourette's as a separate condition, although by no means always, so it is easy to see how the symptoms blur.

Obsessive-compulsive disorder (OCD)

OCD is also commonly associated with Tourette's and may appear before overt tics or even as the only manifestation of someone with the TS genes.

In Tourette's, it is sometimes difficult to separate OCD from some motor tics, especially in a child who may find it difficult to describe why they need to repeat the action. Generally speaking, someone affected by OCD experiences anxiety that is improved by completing the action, usually with a certain number of repetitions that they must count or note.

Angelica describes a level of anxiety building in her chest before she performs a compulsive behaviour such as touching her feet against the door frame.

By comparison, when she tics there is more of a sense of physical irritation and the number of times she repeats the action can be random and varies.

Getting a specialist medical diagnosis – it really isn't all about swearing

Even today, the misconception that coprolalia is a key feature of Tourette's is widespread among clinicians, so more subtle tics such as repetitive blinking or throat clearing may be missed or dismissed.

Even once a referral has been made and Child and Adolescent Mental Health Services (CAMHS) have responded and set an assessment date, getting the right diagnosis may not be easy, and this is the first stage on the path to appropriate treatment. There are very few Tourette's specialists in the UK, and even fewer are attached to local children's services.

The most recently updated (October 2021) directory in the UK listed just 22 medical consultants specialising in Tourette's Syndrome and working in the NHS who offer appointments to children and teens. These are heavily London-centric; Scotland and Northern Ireland boast one each, Wales has none. Central England is slightly anomalous with two child specialists and a further two adult specialists who offer a second opinion for children, but the region includes two major research centres for Tourette's[1].

Angelica first displayed features of OCD in the last year of primary school, and a 'wrinkling her nose' tic. Having already received the Tourette's diagnosis for our son, we pressed for an assessment. A clinical psychology assessment was offered relatively early after five months, but the working diagnosis was OCD, and she was referred for cognitive behavioural therapy (CBT). She started this approximately 15 months after our initial GP referral was made, but it quickly became apparent that her compulsive actions had more features of tics than true compulsions.

It was at my suggestion that her CBT therapist asked for a Tourette's assessment which was eventually offered seven months later, by which time she was in Year 8 of secondary school. At this point, she was still misdiagnosed (by local services), as her mild 'coughing' tic was not picked up and classified as a vocal tic, so she was classified as only having motor tics and a diagnosis of 'complex tic disorder' rather than TS.

A Danish study that looked at delays in diagnosis of Tourette's amongst children found limited knowledge among health professionals as well as the public led to an average duration of 2.8 years from tics developing to diagnosis[2].

In countries with other healthcare systems (such as the US), where families can go directly to a specialist, this initial gate-keeping step may be missed out, thereby speeding up the process. However, the risk then is that without an initial diagnosis, the wrong specialist may be accessed. One of my survey respondents illustrated this problem:

"They tried to take me to the doctor, but they took me to the wrong one." (Delilah, 14, US)

This may lead either to an incorrect diagnosis, or to the child being referred on to further specialists, going yet further off track.

Impact of the COVID-19 pandemic

Whilst it is well recognised that many people's mental health has suffered during the pandemic and associated lockdowns and economic uncertainty, cases of Tourette's have also been reported in unprecedented numbers amongst children and teenagers. As well as reports and articles in the press[3], medical and psychological journal papers have confirmed this to be the case across Europe. New cases emerged weekly during this period, in older children and amongst teenage girls in particular[4]. Many acute-onset cases received a medical diagnosis of functional tics rather than Tourette's. However, in children and adolescents already recognised to have Tourette's, there is increasing evidence that the pandemic has caused worsening of symptoms, especially motor tics, RAGE attacks and associated problems such as anxiety and increased ADHD[5].

In Angelica's case, her previously mild motor tics increased exponentially into florid motor and vocal tics following the combined stress of GCSE mock exams taken within weeks of returning to school after the second lockdown, shortly followed by the third lockdown.

Why this should be the case is not yet understood, but this has enormous implications for medical diagnostic services and educational psychology services.

Mental health services have long been described by those working in the NHS as a 'Cinderella specialty', i.e. working hard for minimal recognition and at the bottom of the funding pile.

Children's mental health services in particular have struggled to keep up, and the associated professions of clinical and educational psychology have been hugely pared back through successive 'service improvements' (or 'cuts' in plain English) amongst NHS trusts and local education authorities.

Well before the pandemic worsened the situation, in 2017–18 the vast majority of NHS clinical commissioning groups in the UK did not know how many young people were waiting for assessment or treatment for mental health issues[6].

Even where people have the means to pay for these services privately, there is a significant waiting list because there are simply not enough trained people working in any particular geographical area.

This situation is not unique to the UK. A survey of parents in Denmark[7] found that children could wait years to access the right help for mental health issues, including neurodevelopmental conditions. Important factors in the Danish survey that influenced how quickly support was accessed were:

- how quickly parents recognised the problem
- how they felt about 'labelling' their child
- how much they pushed health professionals for a referral

In practical terms, this means there are not enough trained staff to either conduct clinical assessments of your child or delineate their schooling support needs to come up with a special educational needs and disability (SEND) statement.

You may need to become a 'pushy parent' whether you like it or not.

Treatment for Tourette's

For most youngsters with Tourette's, treatment is largely reassurance and explanation, emotional support, and a variety of behavioural therapies. I have included a short section on drug treatments and emerging electrical approaches at the end of this chapter, but I want to stress that most children with TS **do not** need them.

Behavioural treatments

A wide range of treatments has been tried to help manage tics in TS and the symptoms of OCD[8]. The most effective approaches to managing tics, according to controlled trials, are: habit reversal training (HRT) with its expanded version, comprehensive behavioural intervention for tics (CBiT), and exposure with response prevention (ERP). Cognitive behavioural therapy (CBT) is a recognised treatment for OCD as well as anxiety, a well-known tic-exacerbating factor.

Habit reversal training (HRT)

This approach to the treatment of tics has been around since the 1970s[9]. Habit reversal concentrates on making the person consciously aware of the repetitive behaviour (awareness training (AT)) and then replacing it with something less bothersome (competing response training (CRT)). For example, when our son had the tic that caused him to fling out his arm and hurt his elbow, habit reversal might have taught him to put his hand on his hip and press until the tic urge ebbed away. This approach can be applied to each tic in turn. Each training session is conducted by a trained therapist, but ongoing social support is also key, with the therapist teaching a parent or carer specific strategies.

Comprehensive behavioural intervention for tics (CBiT)

Whilst HRT is the best studied and most widely used approach, more recently it has been expanded alongside other therapies in an approach called **comprehensive behavioural intervention for tics (CBiT)**. The key additional feature in CBiT is the functional intervention (FI) step. The goal here is to identify environmental or day-to-day factors that worsen tics for the individual and then to change those situations to make tics less likely to occur. This might involve learning methods for stress management or something as simple as introducing activity breaks into a sedentary working day. This has been published in manual form for professionals, parents and young adults with TS[10].

This strategy is described more fully on the Tourettes Action website[11] and in a guide published by the Tourette Association of America[12].

A scientific review that looked at trials comparing several behavioural approaches found that both HRT and CBiT had a medium-sized effect on improving tics[13]. A key point is that these approaches can be hard work and require motivation on the part of the child.

> *Angelica was offered CBT, but because it was aimed at her OCD symptoms rather than her tics, which were mild at the time, she was not particularly motivated to practise after each session.*

But if practised properly, behavioural methods are at least as effective as medication in managing mild to moderate tics (which is the focus of this book) without any of the associated side effects.

Recent research using dynamic MRI scanning has shown that the teenage brain is especially 'plastic'[14], therefore training at this stage can be particularly useful to prevent tics worsening or persisting into adulthood. This reinforces my initial point about the importance of obtaining an early diagnosis.

However, even once diagnosed, the lack of appropriately trained behavioural therapists means that less than 20% of children who are diagnosed get offered CBiT at present[13].

Exposure with response prevention (ERP)

In this approach, the individual learns to suppress their tics (response prevention) while tolerating the urge to tic (exposure). This differs from HRT and CBiT in that no competing response is taught, so potentially reducing the requirement for therapist involvement.

Until very recently this approach had not been well evaluated, so it was not known if it was effective treatment for tics in comparison with the active behavioural methods described above.

However, a recent trial in the UK examined the effectiveness of online remote behavioural intervention for tics (ORBIT)[15]. This trial set out to establish if a therapist-guided, parent-assisted, internet-based behavioural therapy approach focussing on ERP would be acceptable to young people with TS and help them to manage their tics. The results show that ERP is effective in children and adolescents and can be successfully delivered in a remote format with minimal therapist contact time[16]. This potentially offers huge improvements in accessibility to treatment for tics, removing geographical constraints and reducing waiting times.

Medication

Firstly, most children with Tourette's **do not need** medication.

Secondly, because TS is a condition that involves short-circuiting of impulses in an otherwise healthy brain, **medication does not make any difference to the condition itself**. It is used primarily to reduce the severity of tics when they are causing distress or physical harm, or to help with the symptoms of associated conditions like OCD, ADHD or anxiety and depression.

Which drugs can help?

Anti-psychotics

The main drugs used traditionally in Tourette's are neuroleptic tranquillisers (originally developed to treat serious psychotic illnesses such as schizophrenia and mania). These drugs work by blocking dopamine receptors in the brain.

In the early days, the first choice was haloperidol. This was followed by pimozide and more recently second-generation drugs, such as risperidone.

For TS, these drugs are used in much smaller doses than for psychosis, but they still come with several side effects which limit their usefulness. The most common side effects are neurological, particularly sudden muscular stiffness (known as acute dystonia), shaking and restlessness. These side effects usually improve when treatment is stopped.

However, there are less common but more serious side effects. Pimozide causes fewer neurological problems and for a while was preferred over haloperidol, but it can cause potentially fatal heart rhythm changes, so children prescribed it need to have regular ECG (heart) monitoring. Second-generation drugs like risperidone have fewer neurological side effects and are less likely to cause heart problems. However, they can cause weight gain and abnormal sugar and fat metabolism, so need to be used alongside regular monitoring of weight, blood pressure and blood glucose levels.

There is now a third generation of antipsychotic drugs: the main one used for TS is aripiprazole. It appears to be effective in controlling tics through a unique action of both stimulating and blocking dopamine receptors according to how much naturally occurring dopamine is present. It seems to have fewer side effects across the board, making it both lower risk and more acceptable to the young person taking it.

Due to the side effects of all these drugs, they tend to be used only when tics become disabling. They will often be prescribed to young people for a relatively short period, until a particular tic either fades away or is replaced by another that is less distressing.

Alpha agonists

This title simply means a different class of drug in terms of how it works. Alpha agonists include clonidine and, more recently, guanfacine. These have been less widely used than anti-psychotic drugs, despite having fewer side effects, as they tended to be considered less effective, but it is now recognised that this is related to the age at which they are prescribed, being more helpful in children than adults. A systematic review in 2016 found them to be as effective as other drug groups, suggesting that they should be used more often as first-line medication[13], especially in children with both TS and ADHD.

Selective serotonin reuptake inhibitors (SSRIs)

This group of drugs was developed to treat depression. They work by reducing the reuptake and breakdown of the hormone serotonin (the 'happy' hormone) in the brain. The level of this hormone is lower in people with depression, so keeping it higher helps to enhance mood. The drug most commonly used is sertraline.

In TS it is largely used to treat associated problems rather than tics themselves, namely obsessive-compulsive symptoms, depression and anxiety.

Psychostimulants

These are used for symptoms of ADHD rather than Tourette's alone. The most used drug in this group is methylphenidate (commonly known under the brand name of 'Ritalin'). It is important to note that methylphenidate can make tics worse, so should be used with caution for Tourette's. This also emphasises the need for accurate diagnosis.

More information about these medications can be found in other sources, such as the national TS association websites. I have listed the main associations at the back of this book in the Resources section.

The main takeaway point here is that most people with Tourette's **do not take regular medication, and many will not need it at all**. For those that do, it is usually a question of weighing up the benefits for that individual at that time in terms of tic suppression versus the 'cost' of side effects. Medication should **only be prescribed by specialists**.

Physical and electrical treatments

Earlier attempts to control tics included direct surgical 'ablation' (removal) of brain tissue in the 1960s, and more recently, deep brain stimulation. This approach was introduced in 1999 and involves surgical implantation of a device directly into the brain to deliver electrical impulses[17]. Any neurosurgical approach carries significant risk and has therefore been used mostly as a last resort in adults with disabling tics.

However, early results are emerging of a simple but potentially highly effective new treatment that is easy to use and does not carry any surgical risks. The University of Nottingham in the UK recently published a study demonstrating significant reductions in both motor and vocal tics through applying rhythmic electrical current to the median nerve in the wrist via a simple watch-style device that can be controlled by the wearer[18].

For the minority of young adults whose tics do not subside as they get older, this could be a game-changer.

Chapter 3: Parent Action Points – 6-point checklist for getting an expert-led medical diagnosis	
1	Tics can emerge in pre-school or early primary-school children onwards. ADHD or OCD can either exist in their own right or be associated with TS. Make notes or video any behaviours you or your child do not understand, or think could be a tic.
2	Write down when it first started, how long it has been going on, and how the tics or behaviours have changed over time – this is key to getting the correct diagnosis.
3	Take your child to their GP (face to face or remotely) sooner rather than later and explain the situation.
4	Ask for a referral to CAMHS. Some regions will accept self or parent referral, but the GP route is most common.
5	If it is clear to you that your child has multiple tics, look up Tourette's Syndrome and/or Movement Disorder clinics and ask your GP for a direct referral to your nearest regional centre. This may take longer than a referral to CAMHS but ensures that your child is seen by an appropriate specialist from the outset.
6	Don't take no for an answer.

CHAPTER 4

Connect and Collaborate

Tourette's at School

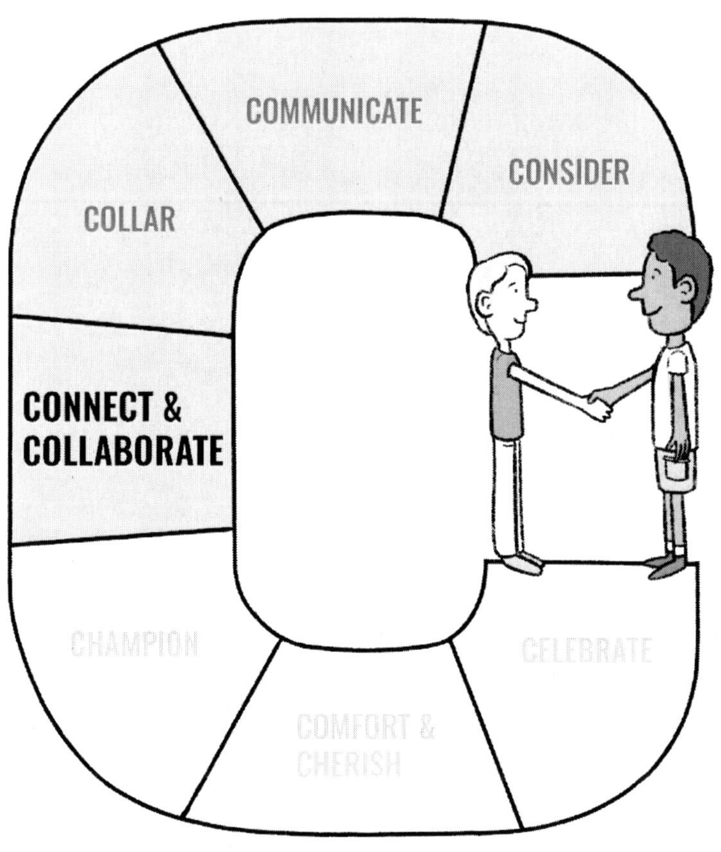

CHAPTER 4

Connect and Collaborate

Tourette's at School

One of the most important and positive actions you can take as a parent of a child with Tourette's is to get in contact with your child's school as soon as you recognise a problem (or as soon as your child tells you that they have a problem). Because Tourette's varies so much in how it shows up in individual children, very few teachers will pick it up, or if they recognise that there is a problem, they are unlikely to understand what it is or how to handle it.

Tics in school

In a younger child who is unable to suppress their tics, many misunderstandings can arise in the primary-school setting (UK system, age 4–11, Foundation Phase to Year 6), such as:

- interpreting motor tics as 'fidgeting' or signs of ADHD
- interpreting vocal tics as being 'chatty', 'noisy' or 'disruptive'

Because the tics themselves evolve and change, they are also less likely to be recognised.

In the secondary school setting (UK system, age 11–18, Years 7–13), we have found that whilst most learning support departments these days are set up for working with children with well-recognised conditions such as dyslexia, and to some extent autism spectrum disorder, they are still largely unaware or unsure of how to cope with children with Tourette's. In the state school system, they have no option to refuse admission, but private schools may decide they are not set up to support children with Tourette's and deny entry altogether.

> *We decided to send Alex to a small independent day school renowned for excellent pastoral care, as we were concerned that he might be bullied in a large comprehensive. Unbeknown to us, staff representatives visited his primary school to check on how problematic his TS was in the classroom. We were only made aware of their concern because his primary-school teachers told us about the visit.*

In an older child, the same issues can arise, but the child may make more effort to suppress their tics, so they are less evident in the classroom. However, this has its own problems.

Tics are exhausting; suppressing tics is also exhausting. Tics can be 'set off' by other people imitating them, consciously or unconsciously.

There can also be occasions when a tic gets **'stuck'**. For a vocal tic, this can appear similar to a stutter; whereas in a motor tic, the child can tense up and be unable to move.

> *When Angelica gets a 'stuck tic', she tenses up her arms, neck and head, and may remain in this position for up to 30 seconds.*

It is imperative that teachers understand what is causing these behaviours.

Simple actions like the student being given a pass to leave the class without challenge and go to a quiet room when their tics become overwhelming can make an enormous difference.

Amongst our survey responders, the majority (12 out of 14) said their school recognised their Tourette's, but even then, some individual teachers were unhelpful:

> ***"My teacher made me feel embarrassed on online classes, I felt terrible." (Sophie, Poland)***

> ***"I've been told to shut up a lot." (Kitty, 16, UK)***

> ***"being told off, mocked (by teachers as well as students)." (Holly, 16, UK)***

Another made the point that, although their main subject teachers were aware of their tics, there had been:

> *"incidents with relief teachers and other teachers not being aware" (Bailey, 17, Australia)*

This has also been our experience:

> *Angelica has had to explain to passing teachers why she is outside her classroom when she's having a tic attack – this became more frequent during the pandemic as students' movements were restricted to maintain class 'bubbles'.*

School in the COVID-19 pandemic

With the shutdown of many schools during the COVID-19 pandemic, teachers and students had to adapt to a range of technologies to provide online teaching and studying at home.

Children with Tourette's experienced a range of positive and negative aspects of remote working, especially when dealing with their tics (which may have either increased in severity due to the wider stresses of the pandemic or emerged for the first time).

Plus points of remote learning

- Because they are online, they can mute themselves so vocal tics are less obvious
- Physical tics can be more easily disguised as only the upper half of the body is visible
- Teachers and fellow students are less likely to pay attention to separate student views, as opposed to noticing the student in the classroom

Minus points of remote learning

- The child is less likely to contribute to any questions and answers or discussion in the class for fear of ticcing, which may then be interpreted as a lack of engagement
- Chunks of the lesson get missed whilst the child is ticcing

Angelica found online teaching exacerbated her tics. She also had to work harder to listen as her tics disrupt her concentration, so she missed what the teacher was saying.

Although the online teaching day had the usual breaks – half an hour each for mid-morning and lunch, by not requiring movement between classrooms, there was less decompression time between lessons. By lunchtime, she was exhausted.

Simple actions can help, such as asking (email on their behalf if the student feels unable to ask) the teacher to keep previous slides or discussion available to view so that, without having to ask, the student can scroll back to check on points that may have been missed.

Since schools returned to face-to-face classroom-based teaching, children with TS (whether previously diagnosed or newly emerging) have needed to find new ways of coping in the classroom environment.

Angelica was given permission to leave the classroom if her tics became overwhelming, but she didn't have anywhere to go.

Clearly, struggling with concentration and trying to suppress tics in the classroom environment can affect learning and information processing. Students with TS may need to work through classroom notes in greater detail afterwards. It is helpful if teachers can acknowledge this:

> ***"My lecturers understand that I get exhausted from college as it makes me tic a lot so they give me extensions on my assignments."*** ***(Grace, 17, UK)***

Because of the lack of educational psychology services, it is falling to parents and teachers to come up with methods for helping children to cope.

On the positive side, both teachers and students have become increasingly aware of how much the pandemic has affected them in terms of their mental health.

Advice for teachers from a student with Tourette's

Cece aka 'Otters Have Pockets' is a relative newcomer to the social media scene (see Chapter 7 for more examples). She is an eloquent UK-based 18-year-old (in 2022) and has the following suggestions for teachers[1]:

1. Ask the student [with TS] how they want people to react to their tics, i.e. take no notice vs laughing with them (not at them) if they are saying funny things

2. Ask the student what kind of things help them and then implement them in the classroom, e.g. allow them to listen to music on headphones to help them to block out classroom noise and concentrate on a task

3. If the student is overwhelmed by tics or sensory stimuli, set up somewhere they can go and take time out

4. Educate themselves [the teacher] on TS, so they can help the student with TS and also educate other students
5. Never single the student out or tell them off for ticcing
6. Never tell them to be quiet (unless they are talking on purpose – the difference is usually clear)
7. Give the student with TS the chance to do a presentation about it to educate the class, but do not force them
8. Students with TS may work differently from their classmates – allow them to go at their own pace
9. Let the student with TS know that their [the teacher's] classroom is a safe space, and that they can come to them with fears or concerns

I can't put it better than that.

You may need to offer some suggestions to the school as to what help your child needs, but with increased post-pandemic awareness, you will be pushing at an open door.

Who to approach at school

The key person to reach is the SENCo (Special Educational Needs Coordinator) as they can initiate not only formal assessments of what is needed at the classroom level (see Chapter 5 for further discussion of examinations) but can also ensure that other teachers are made aware of your child's needs and individual wishes.

In addition, most large secondary schools have a designated support centre or rooms where the student can go if they need to take time out.

Tics and social integration

For many children with Tourette's, school can be a very isolating experience, especially if they already struggle with low self-esteem or social anxiety[2].

Particularly in adolescence, when the desire to be accepted by peers is greatest, they can feel like *'a freak'*.

There is a balance to be struck between not singling them out and improving awareness.

One survey responder suggested she could give a presentation at school to remind people that they should treat her *"like everyone else"*, whilst another thought that the school could talk to people more about it.

Students with TS can also feel conscious of not wanting to disrupt classes. One survey responder said that her school was very accommodating, but she still felt she had to suppress her tics:

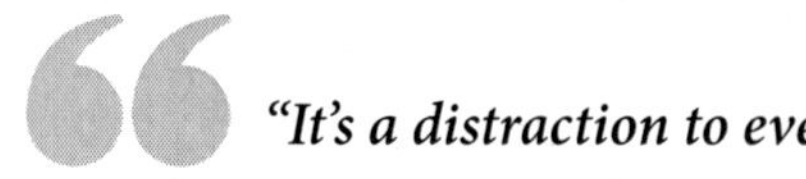

Even if they are confident within their own social grouping, participation in group activities can be fraught with difficulty.

> *Alex struggled with games like football in primary school – he would fall over his own feet when he tried to run or kick the ball. It is only now I can see that it was linked to his tics – he would kick his leg back and upwards when walking along the street.*

FOOTBALL FAILURE

Some schools deal with this issue simply but effectively by allowing students to self-select into 'participation' or 'performance' groups during physical education lessons. This allows kids who are serious about their sports to work with their peers and stops them from getting frustrated, whilst the kids who for any reason struggle with sports can relax and enjoy themselves in a group without feeling judged.

As Alex got older and his tics improved, he was able to take up sports, but he avoided any 'team' games that put peer pressure on him to perform. He enjoyed kung fu at a club outside school and latterly mixed martial arts at university; both provide a great energy outlet and help his balance.

Bullying

This can be an issue for children with TS. It most commonly takes the form of teasing and other children deliberately setting off a child's tic or OCD behaviour, or excluding them from peer groups.

Angelica described how a boy in her class who sat at the same table for group activities noticed her 'stroking the surface of the table'. He would then repeat the action himself, knowing that it would provoke the same repetition in her.

In this instance, once it was pointed out, the teacher took simple remedial action by moving the offender to a different table.

For some, teasing is transient:

"I have had teasing when people first saw me ticcing after we went back to school after the pandemic calmed down but that stopped when people realised it wasn't a big joke." (Mills, 16, UK)

It can also be related to the common perception that they are faking:

"I have been called names like 'chicken' and there have been multiple times where people have said I'm faking." (Elise, 13, US)

Teasing can also be carried out through misunderstanding rather than malice. Sometimes it is the teen's own friends who provoke tics:

"Friends copy my tics to trigger them because they think it's cute." (Kitty, 16, UK)

On the positive side, Generation Z[3] has moved on enormously, embracing inclusivity and diversity in ways that put older generations to shame.

Angelica has developed a close group of friends who all understand her Tourette's. One friend carefully moves all pencils or implements to her side of the table when they work together in class as she knows that when Angelica tics, she will fling these items off the table if they are in reach.

THAT'S WHAT FRIENDS ARE FOR

Angelica also has a particularly tolerant friend whom she can punch when she tics!

	Chapter 4: Parent Action Points – 4-point checklist to support your child in school.
1	Seek out the SENCo at your child's secondary school, even if your child has not been formally assessed or diagnosed. Use them as the primary point of contact to communicate with teachers throughout the school.
2	If your child is working online at home, check what helps or hinders them, make a list, and ensure the school is aware of any difficulties. Follow up to see what action has been taken.
3	If your child is back in the classroom, discuss with them what helps or hinders them (use Cece's list as a guide), then make sure the school knows about it and agrees a plan of action.
4	If your child is being teased or bullied by other students or told off by teachers, take it to the SENCo to discuss the most effective ways of dealing with it. Check back in with your child and follow up if necessary.

CHAPTER 5

Champion Your Child's Future

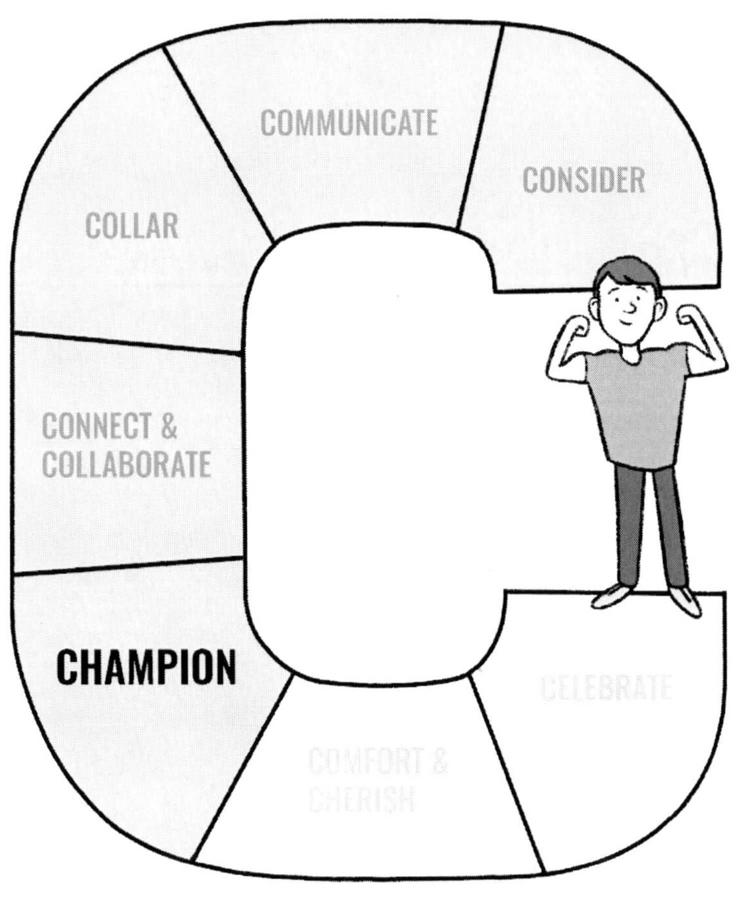

CHAPTER 5

Champion Your Child's Future

Recognising additional educational needs

It is not over-dramatising to say that, without recognition of additional educational needs, a child with Tourette's may end up with educational qualifications that fall way below their actual ability.

Of course, there are lots of examples of successful people who left school with next to no qualifications (Sir Richard Branson to name just one), but there **is a difference between kids with an 'entrepreneurial' spirit who do not fit into a narrow educational model, and those who feel stupid and a failure because no one recognises their struggles**. It is much easier to walk away from a conventional career path when you have self-belief.

Whether or not your child is drawn to academic subjects, they must still deal with assessments during their school career. In the skill-based technical subjects, they are more likely to be assessed based on a portfolio (such as in art or design) or course projects (such as in ICT (information and communications technology) or electronics) but there is still written work to be completed and deadlines to meet. And for most further education courses, there is a minimum requirement of GCSEs in 'core' subjects, usually maths and English.

If they aspire to sixth form and higher education, they must achieve a minimum entry requirement. At present, that's usually five GCSEs at level 5 or above in the numerical grading system of 9–1 introduced in the UK in 2017 (technically level 4 is acceptable as it represents a low 'C' in the old A*–E system, but a lot of sixth form colleges now set the bar at level 5). These must include maths and English, plus subjects relevant to their A-level choices.

However, in some ways it does not matter what results they need. If school has become a stressful drag and assessments a nightmare, they will leave as early as they can, traumatised and unable to view any future possibilities.

As a parent, you are treading a thin line, not wanting to be a 'helicopter' (hovering over your child and teachers) yet wanting to ensure that they can achieve their best potential. Your child may already have low self-esteem and anxiety because of their TS; they are not going to ask for the help they need on their own. They may not thank you for 'making a fuss' at the time, but trust me, one day they will realise how important it was (although they still won't thank you!)

If you have open communication with your child, you can see or find out how they are dealing or struggling with different aspects of their schoolwork and can then bring this to the school's attention.

Crossover with obsessive-compulsive disorder (OCD) in the school setting

In the educational setting, a child with features of OCD alongside their Tourette's can find it difficult to complete timed tasks. This is made worse if the task is any form of 'official' assessment as the anxiety this produces increases both tic frequency and OCD[1].

Alex's maths teacher tried to explain the exam tactic of tackling questions strategically by looking through the paper for the ones where the answers were obvious and answering those first. However, Alex's OCD meant that he found it impossible to switch from one question to another; he had to complete each one in turn and would get stuck and be unable to finish the paper. What he needed was a chance to break from the paper, reset and then start another question.

Dysgraphia and overwriting

Dysgraphia is a relatively uncommon but recognised feature of Tourette's[2], although it can also exist in its own right. It is the neurological 'twin' of dyslexia but affects writing rather than reading.

The signs of dysgraphia include difficulties with:

- forming letters
- writing grammatically correct sentences
- spacing letters correctly
- writing in a straight line
- holding and controlling a writing tool
- writing clearly enough to read back later
- writing complete words without skipping letters

This results in the child's writing progressively deteriorating over time. Some difficulties may be subtle, with the writing style itself unimpaired. For example, the child struggles to hold a pen for longer periods (they may be seen shaking their hand because it has cramped up).

It can be further complicated in Tourette's by OCD in which the child also has a compulsion to write over the same words multiple times (overwriting). This both slows them down and makes their writing illegible. Students with dysgraphia may also struggle to write and listen at the same time, so note-taking in class is particularly challenging.

In one class, Angelica was expected to write down a series of questions before answering them. She took so long to write down the questions that she never got to finish the answers.

Overwriting is usually picked up relatively early but is generally mistaken for poor motor control by teaching staff.

Alex was invited to join a 'remedial writing group' at his school. It was only after I compared examples of his handwriting over time and realised it had got steadily worse that it became apparent the problem was more subtle.

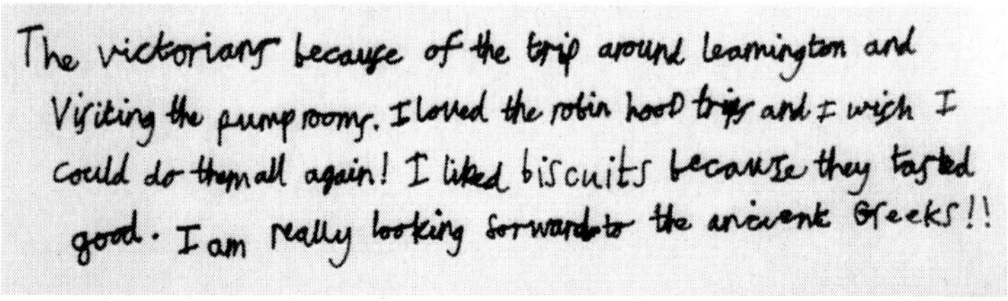
The victorians because of the trip around leamington and Visiting the pump rooms. I loved the robin hood trips and I wish I could do them all again! I liked biscuits because they tasted good. I am really looking forward to the ancient Greeks!!

Alex's handwriting Year 5 – aged 9

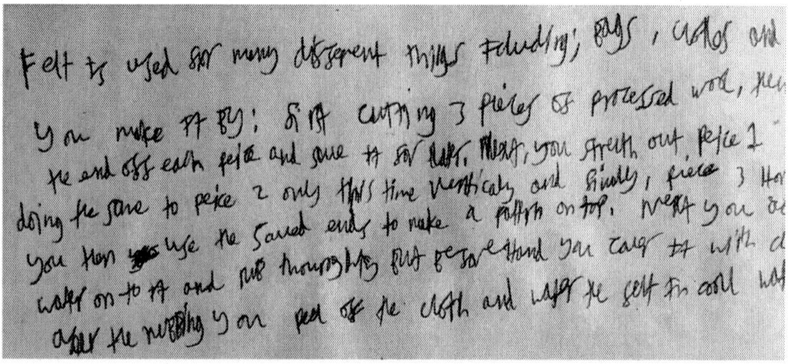

Alex's handwriting Year 8 – aged 12

Tests and examinations

More years ago than I care to remember, I sat my A-levels. I was predicted to get AAB grades in my three subjects and was a firm candidate for medical school (in the days before qualification inflation). However, I had quite severe seasonal hay fever and couldn't take antihistamines as they made me feel sleepy. Instead, I went into every exam with a box of tissues, itchy eyes and throat, a streaming nose, and an urge to sneeze every few minutes. Extra time was unheard of back then, so I rarely finished a whole paper. When the results came out, I had dropped to BCC. (I eventually got into medical school through the 'clearing' system, but that's another story).

Now imagine being a student with Tourette's, who is already stressed by the exam, who feels an overwhelming urge to tic which equates to a physical irritation like needing to sneeze, who is in an exam hall with a hundred others and is acutely conscious of not wanting to distract their classmates, whose hand has cramped up from overwriting and who has already used up half their time going over and over the same question because their OCD has kicked in. How would you do?

Dysgraphia becomes more marked the longer the passage of writing required and the more stress the child is under, so the worst-case scenario is a timed essay or exam.

Alex learned to compensate by writing as succinctly as possible; this was a positive when it came to essay-writing assignments for English language but did not help him in timed examinations with set answer requirements.

The tipping point was when he took two GCSEs a year early, before his needs were fully recognised. For one which required only short-sentence answers, he got an A. However, the other required long paragraphs of continuous writing, and although he was allowed to use a computer keyboard because his writing was so illegible, he had no additional time to compensate for his slow typing speed, let alone the effect of stress on his compulsion to backspace and overtype. Despite having done well in his coursework and been predicted an A grade, under timed conditions he came out with a D.*

At this point, I approached his Tourette's specialist to send further evidence that he had specific educational needs, and his school finally acted and applied for additional 'access arrangements' for exams. Once he was given extra time and *rest breaks in addition to the use of a keyboard, he performed as his coursework predicted in the rest of his GCSEs a year later, obtaining a mix of A*, As and Bs.*

We were lucky that our son was able to take some exams early. If he had done them all at the same time without additional support, his outcomes could have been much lower.

What are access arrangements and how do they help?

Exam access arrangements are defined as reasonable adjustments for candidates who have the required knowledge and skills, but who can't demonstrate this due to their disability. Clearly these arrangements must not affect the overall aim of the examination or give the student an unfair advantage. The individual student requirement for access arrangements must be assessed by appropriately qualified learning support staff and then applied for by the school.

In UK schools, it is the Joint Council for Qualifications (JCQ) that oversees Exam Access Arrangements for GCSE and GCE (A-level) qualifications. They base their decisions on:

- the school's knowledge of the student's needs and support in the classroom – their normal way of working
- finding of an assessor's appraisal
- the requirements of the subjects the student is taking

Crucially, the student does **not** need to have received a formal diagnosis of a learning disability to receive access arrangements, so a medical diagnosis of Tourette's is not essential. However, it will help in putting pressure on the school if they are slow to take things forward.

Exact requirements will vary from child to child but several appear to be consistently helpful for students with Tourette's:

- **A separate room** – this will allow them to tic without worrying about distracting others, which reduces anxiety and in turn reduces tic frequency.
- **Rest breaks** – this is when the clock is 'stopped' for a short period (the number and length of rest breaks are agreed in advance). It can be helpful when tics are becoming overwhelming or when the student with OCD gets 'stuck' and can't progress with the paper. The rest break is supervised (which may include leaving the examination room) and the student doesn't have access to the paper during it. With rest breaks the overall length of the examination remains the same, although it will finish later (a bit like 'injury time' in football matches).
- **Additional time** – for some students rest breaks are sufficient, but others may need extra time. The usual allowance is an extra 25% (so if the paper is two hours, the student will get an extra 30 minutes). The student is allowed to use this time as needed, including to plan their answers at the start of the exam, read through the paper, or read through completed questions.
- **Use of a keyboard** – this is especially helpful for students with dysgraphia who struggle to write.
- **Use of a scribe** (person who is trained to write down the student's verbal responses) – this is needed less often but may be necessary for a student with OCD complicating their Tourette's who struggles to use a keyboard.

Amongst my survey responders, several had sat formal tests or exams, and whilst most of their schools recognised their TS, not all of them had 'access arrangements'. Best cases were where students were allowed to sit tests in a separate room and given rest breaks and extra time. Another was allowed extra time, a laptop and a separate room.

However, another had limited help:

> ***"I was allowed fidgets but would be kicked out if they got loud." (Kathy, 15, US)***

Another said simply:

> ***"I'm honestly not sure how I did it." (Lexi, 14, US)***

It is important to point out to any sceptics that these supports only level the playing field. They do not give the child any unfair advantages.

Subtle tics and processing problems like overwriting can continue to be a problem even when more obvious tics have improved or resolved. This has implications for youngsters moving into sixth form or further education.

> *Alex moved school between GCSEs and sixth form, and his educational support needs somehow failed to transition with him. At his first parents' evening, one of his teachers expressed frustration that he was getting D grades in timed assignments in class, but when asked to repeat them as a remedial task the following day in non-timed conditions, he would get an A or B. It turned out she was unaware that he had specific support needs and arrangements. Once these were put in place he sailed on, eventually passing his A-level in that subject with an A*.*

This was a simple yet clear-cut illustration to us that even the most subtle manifestations of Tourette's can have major implications.

SUCCESS!

Post-pandemic examinations and assessments

When it comes to national level assessments, I am writing this in the unusual circumstances that all GCSEs and A-levels (and equivalent Highers in Scotland) in the UK have been cancelled for two years in a row, in both 2020 and 2021.

This means that whilst students sat assessments, these were guided through local schools, and it was the teachers who submitted their grades, rather than through standardised public examinations.

For students who already had a TS diagnosis and additional access arrangements in place, this will not have changed their circumstances, but for newly emerging cases, teachers may have had to assess students with little notice.

If your child was in an exam year group, this could have important implications for future job and college applications, irrespective of their results. If they did well, it should still be noted that they had unmet learning needs which may require further support in the future. If they did badly, it could influence the likelihood of colleges offering them places for further or higher education despite their previous performance.

Therefore, it is important that if you, as a parent, have observed tics or other behaviours emerging during the various lockdowns, you contact your school's SENCo. Whilst it will not directly affect your child's grades, it could affect how those results are interpreted in the future.

The same applies to students who are due to sit exams in 2022 and after. As the success of vaccination programmes allows the return to national systems and standardised assessments, it becomes even more important that both pre-existing and newly emerging learning needs are recognised and met.

Whatever stage your child is at, the sooner you start connecting and collaborating with the school, the better.

Call for change

There has been a lot of discussion amongst teachers, educationalists and clinicians as to how we should move on from the COVID-19 pandemic.

The emphasis on examination of a few 'core' subjects, a system originally put in place (in the UK) to try and reach a standard view of 15–16-year-olds, has not essentially changed since the General Certificate of Education was implemented in 1947, when most children left school at that age. The core subjects themselves have not been formally reviewed since the School Certificate was introduced in 1918[3].

However, the emphasis on examinations in those core subjects has reduced most schools' capacity to deliver on anything else, especially as funding in real terms for 'optional' subjects has been reduced.

For some children, examinations work well. These are the children who respond to the challenge of short-term deadlines, can memorise large amounts of information (albeit which is unlikely to be retained) and can organise themselves to regurgitate facts in a set order according to the wording of the questions.

However, for children who are academically bright but approach learning in a different way, or have different needs, the examination system is a deeply unfair way of summarising five or more years of learning.

These children like to think things through and overanalyse exam questions, or have information-processing difficulties, or have obsessive-compulsive disorder and struggle to complete a paper, or have tics and are physically exhausted from the effort of getting through an exam.

Even before the pandemic, children in the UK reported increasing levels of emotional distress. In 2017, one in nine children were anxious or depressed – this went up to one in six in 2020[4]. Children from economically deprived backgrounds or those with pre-existing mental health issues have been worst affected.

But for all children, the uncertainty over their schooling has been a huge source of stress.

It would be wonderful if governments could resist imposing top-down changes on the education system, but in the real world, this is unlikely to happen. However, by forcing everyone to explore new ways of working and teaching, the pandemic has potentially opened up opportunities to use new modalities and emphasise different ways of learning.

The best thing that could come out of this would be a return to assessment of learning outcomes that includes a greater emphasis on coursework and student-led projects throughout the year, rather than snapshot examinations. This is the principle of the more 'practical' subjects covered in BTEC (Business and Technology Education Council) qualifications, but the subtext is that this approach is for less 'academic' children. Prior to 2017, it accounted for a relatively high percentage of GCSE and A-level grades as well, but the 'reforms' implemented by Michael Gove (then UK secretary of state for education) put the emphasis back on the end-of-year exams.

I admit to a level of personal bias here, as someone who struggled with examinations both at school and in their professional career. However, I did eventually manage to obtain a Bachelor of Science degree in psychology, a medical degree, a master's degree in clinical education with distinction (based on coursework and a dissertation) and a doctorate of medicine (based on three years of self-originated research and an 85,000-word thesis). I didn't have TS, and I did have self-belief. Ironically, I even ended up helping to design examination papers!

You cannot make your child's Tourette's go away, and you probably can't change the education system singlehandedly, but you can fight your child's corner.

	Chapter 5: Parent Action Points – 5-point checklist to prevent examination disasters
1	Ask your child if they struggle with taking notes or writing, and keep samples of handwriting from primary school to compare with later.
2	If your child has had a medical diagnosis of TS, send copies of the report to the school. Whilst it is not a requirement for obtaining exam access arrangements, it will guide the school assessor and strengthen your child's case.
3	Keep up the pressure via the SENCo to get your child assessed for additional access arrangements for any formal assessments, whether in school or public examinations.
4	Check with individual teachers that they know what extra support your child needs in the classroom for any formal assessments.
5	If your child has been assessed and changes school, make sure the new school is aware of your child's access arrangements – don't assume they've been told.

CHAPTER 6

Comfort and Cherish

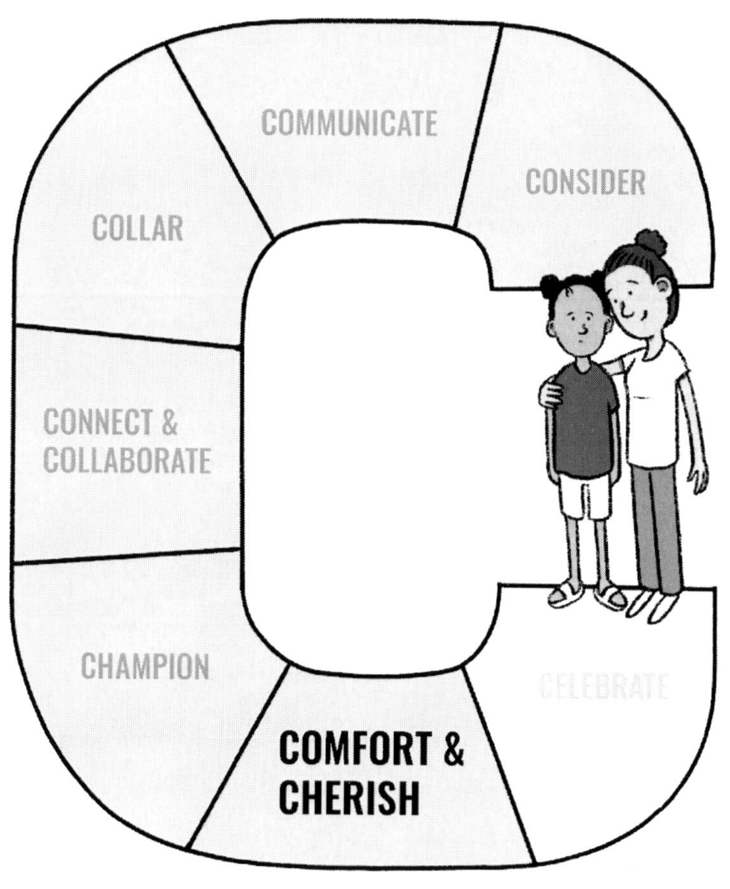

CHAPTER 6

Comfort and Cherish

A place of sanctuary

As a school-age child and especially as a teen, the desire to be accepted by one's peers is a large part of emotional well-being. One of the difficulties for many young people with TS is feeling isolated from both their peers and their families[1].

The fact that Tourette's often emerges during the primary and early secondary school years means that children with TS are trying to learn to deal with the many ways in which their condition can present alongside all the other trials of puberty and adolescence, such as body image, mood swings, tiredness – the list goes on.

As a parent or carer, you cannot always protect your child, as much as you might want to.

What you can do is offer a place of comfort and acceptance for what they are going through.

The single most useful thing you can do is to make home a place of sanctuary and no judgement.

Tics can be physically uncomfortable and exhausting, but they can also be funny. It is okay to laugh **with** your child, as long as it's not **at** them.

Angelica describes her tics as a separate persona called Eve. Angelica's personality is quiet and shy, but Eve is a mischievous sprite, who enjoys slapping her father on the forehead (actually Angelica does too!)

SPLAT!

Emotional support

This may be just providing a listening ear, as you would for any child. Let them tell you how it feels for them, and what they are experiencing, without you feeling that you have to fix it for them. For kids with TS, being able to be themselves at home goes a long way to maintaining and boosting their self-esteem.

It is terribly sad that many youngsters report their families dismiss their tics as nervous habits or attention-seeking behaviour, which forces them to suppress at home. Your child with TS may be 'different' from the rest of the family (or not, if you have more than one child with TS).

How you make them feel about that is up to you.

Informational support

Once you have acknowledged that your child has TS, there is a wealth of information out there; you just have to look for it.

The best resources are the national association websites. The Tourette Association of America is the oldest organisation having been founded in the 1970s, followed not long after by the Tourette Syndrome (UK) Association, which was set up in 1980, and became Tourettes Action in 2008. In both cases the original impetus came from small groups of parents of children with TS. However, they grew rapidly, are now supported by health professionals and are responsible for inspiring ground-breaking research. They also set out and signpost emotional and practical support, and provide tools for children, parents, teachers and health professionals alike.

Many other countries have followed suit, but if your location does not have its own association, there is still a wealth of relevant information to be found on the US and UK association websites.

If you ensure that you are informed, you are in a much better position to support your child, whether that means just understanding their behaviour better, or to tackle outside organisations.

For example, in my survey, one respondent described the way her parents helped her day to day:

"[they] always make sure I have what I need and are always researching/coming up with ideas to make my tics more bearable and less irritating." (Lexi, 13, US)

Other respondents referred more to their parents helping in external situations:

"...they stand up for me whenever I can't stand up for myself." (Bailey, 17, Australia)

"[they] advocate for me." (Kathy, 15, US)

To give you a starting point, I have included a 'References and Resources' section at the end of this book, which includes the research papers and documentaries I have quoted, and the web addresses of the main associations.

Music for the soul

Many youngsters with Tourette's find music helpful in calming their tics. For some this may mean being able to listen on headphones either at home or school.

Others have found that actively playing a musical instrument gives them both an enjoyable pastime and helps control their tics.

This may last for the duration of playing, with the tics returning once the person finishes the piece. This is illustrated brilliantly in a YouTube video of Esha Alwani, a young American woman giving a TED talk about her Tourette's, actively ticcing as she does so. She then sits at the piano and plays and sings one of her own compositions (she started song writing at the age of six). During her performance her tics disappear, but when she finishes and stands to acknowledge the applause, they return[2].

However, the effect of music can be harnessed in a more enduring way. In one fascinating example documented in a BBC TV documentary[3], Greg Storey, a young man in his 20s, describes how learning to play the drums both helped him as a teen and continues to help him as an adult. What is extraordinary in his case is that he has learned how to 'play the drums' in his head to control his tics so effectively that people think they have disappeared altogether, yet they would return within hours if he stopped.

So, if you can, encourage them to play whatever instrument appeals to them.

Keeping safe

Tic attacks

Tics in TS evolve constantly which can cause anxiety. Tic attacks can be especially disturbing both to the young person who has them and to people watching. It is difficult to describe or classify a tic attack because it varies so much between individual people and between individual attacks in any one person. In the medical literature, they are generally described as "disabling bouts of non-suppressible repetitive tics occurring in full consciousness"[4]. This last point is especially important as tics have been mistaken for epileptic seizures.

The research paper quoted above reported tic attacks lasting anything from three minutes to three hours, with provoking factors including increased OCD symptoms and preceding prolonged suppression of tics. In this survey, tic attacks were most experienced by people from 10 to 19 years old and were more likely to occur in people with co-existent ADHD or OCD and with generally more severe TS.

Angelica describes a tic attack starting with a feeling 'like electricity' throughout her body, then she cannot stop moving. This may involve repeating the same tic with particular intensity, or a set of tics.

Tic attacks are especially likely to occur when the person is in stressful circumstances or has had to suppress their tics for a prolonged period.

When Angelica's school observed the two-minute silence at 11 am on Remembrance Day, she was determined to participate, but was extremely anxious about suppressing her tics. She managed to get through it but went on to have a tic attack later that afternoon.

For the young person with TS, it is important to have someone around them who understands what is happening to them when they are having a tic attack, who can just be there and reassure them.

This was reinforced by my survey respondents:

"They [parents] hug me and it calms my tics." (Sophie, Poland)

...although physical restraint is not always helpful.

Holly (16, UK) said, on the one hand, that her parents:

"help me with my tic attacks."

but she qualified this by saying that she would prefer them to:

"not restrain me when I'm having my tic attacks."

Physical support

Sometimes physical tics can take a more subtle form in which the person stops moving completely and freezes. This may occur when they are standing up or cause the person to sit or drop to the ground. It becomes a real problem when the person is in a potentially unsafe location (such as the middle of the road).

TICS CAN BE BADLY TIMED.

Angelica has episodes where her head droops down and forwards and she cannot move. She is fully awake and aware, but she cannot speak or respond to questions. These episodes normally subside spontaneously within a couple of minutes, but she needs an understanding friend or family member physically close by for reassurance.

Obviously, younger children are more likely to be accompanied, but for teens and young adults, it can hugely affect their independence and confidence:

"I don't feel comfortable going anywhere on my own." (Kitty, 16, UK)

Another respondent reported drop attacks and tics affecting mobility:

"I can't be left alone or do basic tasks on my own." (Bailey, 17, Australia)

At other times, physical tics can go beyond uncomfortable to painful or involuntarily self-harming, and then you need some ingenuity.

Damage Limitation

Throwing, hitting or punching tics are not uncommon in Tourette's. They are not usually 'aimed' at anyone or anything but can cause damage or injury. For example, throwing a cup of hot coffee may lead both to breakages and scalding accidents. The practical way of dealing with this is to use a thermos type mug with a sealed lid and flip out sipper (available online or in outdoor camping shops).

Similarly, it is now easy to source shock-absorbent protective phone cases. Again, these were designed largely for outdoor activities, but can avoid a lot of tears (and cost) among young Touretters.

However, sometimes you just need to avoid the situation until the tic fades, or the person learns to suppress. Don't ask your teen with a throwing tic to chop vegetables!

Making self-protection 'cool' – chewellery

One area that has been successful in recognising a need and bringing products to market is the proliferation of online companies selling chew toys for people. These range from simple non-toxic chew toys for young children to aesthetically attractive chewy pendants or 'chewellery'. These were originally produced for children with autism, but the TS community have also found them beneficial for helping to direct biting tics or to reduce anxiety that provokes other tics.

> *Angelica has several chewy pendants in her signature pastel colours which complement her outfits.*

However, it is surprising how few customisable products are available to help kids protect themselves.

> *When I needed a padded hand and wrist support for Angelica to protect her when she hits the side of her hand on the table, all I could find were cycling gloves, but these were padded on the palm. The alternative was all-round thickly padded gloves for gardening or DIY, whereas what she needed was lightweight padding that could be positioned on the side of her hand without affecting her finger movement.*
>
> *What we eventually developed (with the help of a blog post from Touretteshero – see Resources section) was a tubigrip bandage folded in half with small pieces of padding (trimmed from shoulder pads or redundant bras!) tucked between the layers. This provided a practical, albeit unattractive, solution.*

I can't help feeling there must be a pitch in there somewhere for *Dragons' Den*...[5]

Keeping safe with coprolalia

For younger children, coprolalia can be extremely distressing both for parent and child. The child will find themselves saying words that they have heard but barely understand and would never dream of using, and then have to watch the angry or horrified reactions of people around them.

For older teens with Tourette's, this can be especially troublesome when they are outside the home, particularly in settings where they don't know people, such as in the street. Because their language is more developed than younger children, and swearing is more normalised in their age group, their tics are more likely to be misinterpreted as conscious behaviour. In addition, because tics are highly suggestible, a tic may emerge in response to something or someone they have seen or heard in real time and therefore appears to have conscious motivation.

For example, they might pass an overweight man in the street and their tic emerges as, "Fat w*nker, go f*ck yourself".

The more anxious they become, the more likely they are to tic. If your child is going through a significant period of ticcing, it is helpful to connect with organisations such as the police, particularly community support officers who often work with schools. This can help prevent misunderstandings escalating. This was well illustrated in a BBC TV documentary which showed a meeting between a family and their pre-teen son with Tourette's with community police at their local police station. This enabled them to both demonstrate and explain their child's tics[3].

Self-help explanations

Older kids and teens with Tourette's are generally savvier about finding resources for themselves and utilising them.

For example, supermarkets have produced sunflower lanyards to which people can attach 'hidden disability' cards. This took off in part during the COVID-19 pandemic, due to people reporting episodes when they were verbally or even physically abused by other customers or staff for either not wearing a face mask or for not maintaining social distancing.

Several charities, including Tourettes Action, have taken this approach and now produce merchandise to support a wide range of people with hidden disabilities, but kids and teens are also producing and customising their own. Carrying or wearing their lanyards can help explain tic behaviour in public settings. Indirectly, the wearer may also find that their tics diminish as they feel less anxious.

Youngsters are doin' it for themselves

As I have described throughout the book, part of my research came from survey responses from teenagers on the self-administered Uncontrollables Discord server. What comes across very strongly is how isolated these young people can feel, and how much being part of an online support group helps.

What do you find helpful about being in the Server?
The community feeling it brings; if one person says they are struggling, there are always people there to support each other.
Supportive and other people with tics.
Community.
I have made new friends who are very understanding.
I'm not alone anymore.
I find it's helpful because there's a lot of advice on how to deal with tic attacks.
Knowing that I am not alone in managing the TS. Being able to ask for advice. There is a strong sense of community, even if you don't contribute anything.
It's nice to have people with the same experience.
Meeting/talking to others with tics/TS. I don't know anyone IRL [in real life] with tics/TS.
Finding more people to relate to.
Feeling less alone and being able to relate to experiences.

What also comes across very powerfully is their sense of how misunderstood TS is.

What would you like people reading this book to know about TS from your perspective?
Having tics isn't just getting away with swearing in class. It's a daily struggle and people somehow say they want tics. It doesn't make sense to me that people would want to embarrass themselves and hurt themselves without meaning to and be unable to stop it.
It's not a hehe funny joke.
If you see a person ticcing, you shouldn't call them crazy or a freak. Be accepting and understanding.
That it's nothing you can imagine. You will have to experience it to know what we are going through. All the thoughts in our head and how to react to the negative comments that we get on a daily basis.
I want them to know that it's really, really hard. It's not fun or quirky.
How inaccessible healthcare is to some people.
Not all people tic all the time and it doesn't make it any less important even if you think they are 'cute'.
There is a side of TS that most people don't see. Many people just see it as swearing but don't understand the harm it can cause to oneself and the impact that it has on your independence.

The impact of associated problems

Sensory defensiveness

Children with TS can find it difficult to process all the sensory stimuli that are part of normal experience, and this can manifest as both hypersensitivity and hyposensitivity, and include a wide variety of sensory experiences, including touch, taste and sound.

Both Alex and Angelica found loud noise impossible to tolerate. Their primary school held a firework display and social event each year, and whilst they enjoyed meeting up with all their friends and watching the fireworks, they could only stand the noise with earplugs in place and ear defenders over the top.

As Angelica's TS emerged more fully in her teens, she struggled with going to the cinema. She went to see the final episode of the Marvel franchise when her desire not to wait for it to be released on DVD and risk 'spoilers' of the closely guarded ending won out over her physical discomfort; but she had to wear ear defenders to be able to tolerate the volume.

Alongside the other aspects of TS, these difficulties may subside over time, as the teen reaches adulthood, at which point sociability may outweigh sensitivity.

Alex is now in his early 20s and can attend heavy metal gigs, so he has clearly got over his sensitivity to loud noise!

Anxiety

I deliberately did not ask directly about mental health issues in my survey, as I was not in any position to offer help or raise an alarm. However, I did ask if any other features associated with TS were part of the picture, and the range raised by respondents was striking. Not surprisingly, given their known associations with TS, several respondents mentioned ADHD and OCD. ASD was also reported, although in most cases this had yet to be diagnosed.

However the most pervading feature was anxiety; this appeared to be both because of their TS and also contributed to making it worse, which could impact on all activities.

It has long been recognised that people with Tourette's Syndrome find social settings especially anxiety-provoking which worsens their tics, setting up a vicious cycle whereby they start to avoid social interaction, leading to anxiety and depression.

If the young person struggles to control their tics or receives negative comments, it is not surprising that they can end up withdrawing to a safe space. During the pandemic and lockdown, that may mean hiding in their bedroom, or if they do not have a private space, the bathroom.

> ***"Anxiety, it's quite crippling. It's hard to do things." (Holly, 16, UK)***

> ***"Undiagnosed social anxiety. I'm scared to talk to people." (Sophie, Poland)***

> ***"When my anxiety is bad, it stresses me out and makes my tics worse." (Mills, 16, UK)***

Recent studies have found that the neurophysiological changes in the brain when people with TS are asked to look at faces showing different emotions are different from those in people without TS. Their conscious ability to distinguish between different emotions is comparable, but dynamic MRI shows that in people with TS, more neural pathways are involved. What this means is that people with TS have heightened awareness, at an unconscious level, of 'angry' social responses, alongside increased tic provocation[6].

It is not surprising that they can end up hiding away.

Getting a life – a few practical tips

There are times when Tourette's can be hard to live with, not only for the young person themselves, but for family members, whether you feel you understand it or not.

Teens with TS can become very self-absorbed about their tics, especially if these change a lot. Because the tics are so exhausting, this increases the usual adolescent behaviour of sleeping in late.

They may also struggle with all aspects of organisation; getting out of the house for the morning school run is a stressful point for most families, but this can be magnified if a child has TS.

Family gatherings can be a trial, especially if the wider family do not recognise the tics as TS.

Going out can also be difficult, notably in contained social settings such as restaurants or cinemas.

There is often a balance to be struck between becoming socially isolated and adding to both you and your child's stress and distress by exposing them to such situations. However, there are simple steps you can take to reduce everyone's anxiety and enjoy a range of events.

For example, busy restaurants or cafes with lots of background 'hubbub' are generally more family friendly. Those with seating divided into separate cubicles where behavioural tics are less observable and vocal tics harder to locate can help. In good weather, pubs with gardens are an especial godsend. Go during the day or earlier in the evening so your child is not tired. Avoid 'Restaurant Le Posh' (shout out to Horrid Henry fans[7]).

If your child does enjoy cinema and is not sensory overloaded, go for the action-adventure movies where the soundtrack has lots going on. If they are enjoying the film and engrossed in it, they are less likely to tic, but if they do, a 'whoop' during a battle scene is far less noticeable than in a drama.

Sports events like football matches are usually outdoors and noisy, and if your child is a participant rather than a spectator, their tics will usually abate whilst they are concentrating. If you are into fitness yourself, activities like parkrun are brilliantly inclusive (and you don't even have to run – walking is just as acceptable).

Similarly, if you enjoy music events, there are many outdoor festivals (a lot are free to attend) where you can normally move about between several stages. Avoid classical concerts in quiet auditoriums.

For general anxiety, having something as simple as a discreetly hidden 'fidget' toy will often help, as the young person can distract themselves.

> *Angelica has a fidget puzzle toy that she carries with her in a jacket pocket if she's going anywhere new or stressful. She also has special permission to take her plushie 'emotional support' frog into examinations. It fits neatly into the palm of her hand and comforts her if she starts to panic.*

Chapter 6: Parent Action Points	
1	Listen.
2	Avoid judgement.
3	Build time buffers into a normal day to prevent stress all round.
4	Don't avoid family outings but plan ahead to keep the event enjoyable.
5	Encourage your child to challenge themselves physically and socially, but do not force them.
6	There will be times when your teen needs you around to keep them safe but try to offer support on their terms.

CHAPTER 7

Celebrate

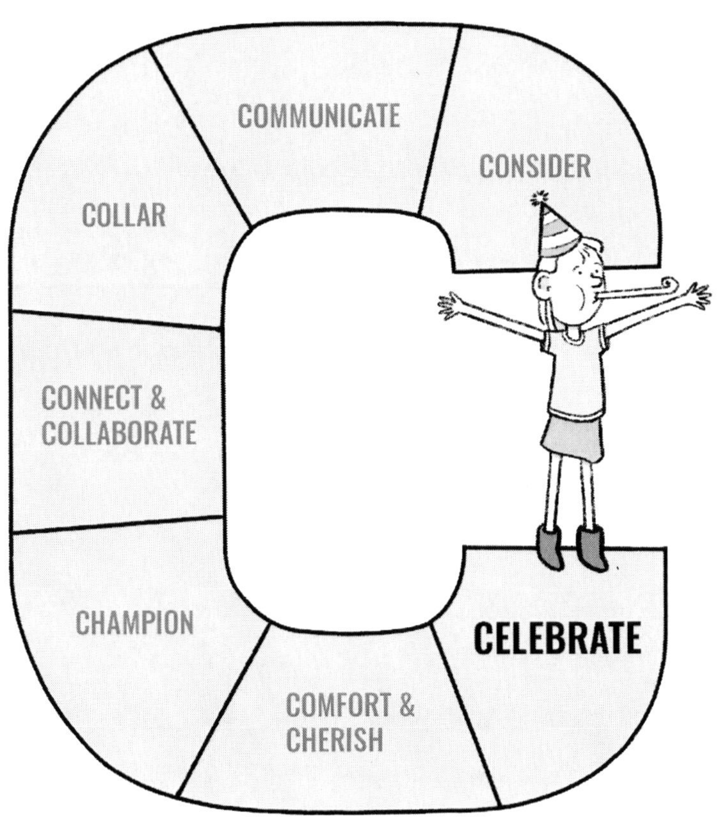

CHAPTER 7

Celebrate

Tourette's Syndrome is a complex and still much misunderstood condition that does **not** affect your child's health, intelligence, physical development or overall learning abilities, yet it is incurable and can be disabling.

However, in the majority of TS cases, the tics either disappear or become easier to manage as the young person moves from adolescence to adulthood and the condition does not prevent them from fulfilling life or career ambitions.

In addition, there is evidence that Tourette's may have some positive effects, and that children with TS may be more gifted than their peers in a range of different areas.

In the 1990s, a new term was coined: twice exceptional (abbreviated to '2e'). This refers to gifted students who have some form of disability. 2e children may have a range of gifts in terms of intellectual, creative, perceptive or motor abilities, alongside neurodevelopmental or learning disabilities that make it difficult for them to learn in a traditional environment[1]. Much of the early emphasis in investigating this concept was on better known disorders such as ADHD and ASD, but Tourette's Syndrome is recognised within that grouping, and attention is turning increasingly towards it.

Recently, a more descriptive term has emerged to remove the stigma associated with neurodevelopmental disorders: 'neurodivergent'.

Neurodivergent simply means 'someone who thinks differently from the way the majority expect'.

In the 2000s, alongside an increased understanding of how brain functioning is altered at a neurobiological level in Tourette's Syndrome, researchers have paid more attention to ways in which these differences may positively affect both creative thinking and performance, rather than just focussing on the negatives.

Several recent scientific studies have found that cognitive control (the process by which goals or plans influence behaviour) is enhanced in young people with Tourette's compared with their peers, because they have learned to suppress their tics[2].

Other studies have shown that children with Tourette's process aspects of language faster, particularly the ability to form sounds into words[3]. This resonates intuitively when you watch TikTok videos of Touretters responding to their audiences, e.g. Sweet Anita (of whom more later).

Whilst it is still early days, it is now recognised that there are multiple avenues for research into how Tourette's may enhance creativity[4].

Adaptability is key to working alongside Tourette's. A good example of this is Greg Storey, a young British man whose ability to control his Tourette's by mentally drumming was described in Chapter 6. Whilst it took him eight years to learn to do this, it also enabled him to follow an entrepreneurial path. Having studied VFX (visual effects) and concept design at college, he went on to work as a freelance designer and set up his own software company, using a language concept he had originally developed as a way of communicating with himself when his Tourette's became overwhelming[5]. The company eventually failed, but undeterred, he turned to broadcasting on Twitch, which he now does full-time as Mrgregles, streaming musical, educational and tech-based content[6].

The UK charity Tourettes Action was able to expand its aims and reach after receiving financial help from Big Brother[7] 2006 winner, Pete Bennett (who also has TS). Tourettes Action stresses the importance of following your dreams and not allowing TS to define you.

Certainly, the responses of my teenage survey group indicate a wide range of hopes and aspirations:

What are you planning or hoping to do in the future?
Costume design and production at university
College to do drama, psychology, and possibly English
Go to college and be a primary-school teacher
Become an author
Theatre or something in the medical field (although I don't want to be involved with surgery or anything)
Be a teacher, a manga artist, an animator, and a freelance artist or designer of some sort
Clinical psychologist or social worker
Social work
Become a geologist
I don't have a solid plan, but I enjoy psychology and art
Go into STEM [science, technology, engineering and mathematics]

This positive message is being further underpinned by people in a wide variety of careers who are opening up about their Tourette's diagnosis, either in the media or by writing books themselves.

Coming out – Celebrities with Tourette's in performing arts and sports

Historically, it has long been debated and disputed that Mozart demonstrated evidence of Tourette's Syndrome alongside his musical creativity and performance genius[8], whilst the English writer Samuel Johnson was documented by contemporaries as having several tics and habits[9].

Although these historical examples cannot be proven, there is a growing list of living performers and other celebrities who have publicly acknowledged their tics or related disorder. These include:

- Dan Aykroyd, US actor and musician
- David Beckham, UK footballer (and national treasure!)
- Jean-Michel Blais, French-Canadian composer and pianist
- Giles Coren, UK food writer and television presenter
- James Durbin, US rock musician
- Billie Eilish, the young US music phenomenon (writer/performer of the Oscar-winning theme song for the James Bond movie *No Time to Die*)
- Jim Eisenreich, US baseball player
- Jamie Grace Harper, US Grammy-nominated musician
- TIX aka Andreas Haukeland, Norwegian musician who wrote and sang Norway's song for Eurovision 2021
- Tim Howard, UK premier league and US national soccer team goalkeeper
- Amir Khan, Singaporean martial arts champion

- Howie Mandel, Canadian comedian, actor, gameshow host and judge on TV show *America's Got Talent*
- Griff McCrary, US teenage golf player
- Dash Mihok, US actor, also a national ambassador for the Tourette Association of America
- Seth Rogen, Canadian stand-up comedian and actor
- Aidy Smith, UK TV presenter and wine and spirits journalist
- Michael Wolff, US jazz pianist and film-score writer (also father of Nat and Alex Wolff – both of whom are actors/ musicians)

Some of these people have largely learned to control their tics, or their movements have naturally subsided with adulthood[10].

However, the list also includes people who work alongside their tics.

Tim Howard is the goalkeeper who had a string of successes with Manchester United and Everton FC in the UK before moving to the US to become the US national team's most capped goalkeeper. He found that whilst his tics were clearly present during a game when the action was at the other end of the pitch, his physical hyper-reactivity came into its own when he was defending his goalmouth. His tics would disappear, he would become totally focussed and his ability to interpret the moves of the striker and react rapidly led to him becoming world-renowned for stopping shots. In one World Cup match (2014, Belgium vs US) he made a record 16 saves.

Michael Wolff, the extraordinary jazz pianist and composer has acknowledged that, whilst he has largely suppressed his tics in adult life, his ability to improvise in his music may be linked to his Tourette's: *"I can go from one thing to the next really fast, and not have to make logical connections"*[11].

TOURETTERS CAN BE EXTREMELY TALENTED!

Whilst none of these extraordinary people would have chosen to have Tourette's, they have managed not only to cope but to excel.

Professional careers

In addition to people demonstrating creative and physical performance abilities in the arts and sports arenas, there are also examples of people who have followed extraordinary professional career paths, despite lifelong Tourette's symptoms.

Dr Dunc

B Duncan McKinlay aka 'Dr Dunc', a Canadian psychologist, has turned his TS into his life's work. After self-diagnosing at the age of 19, he graduated in psychology at McMaster University, Canada, and went on to obtain a doctorate, focussing on educational psychology, clinical psychology and behavioural neuroscience, and is on the faculty of the University of Western Ontario in the departments of psychology and psychiatry. He has authored numerous works[12] and received multiple awards.

In 2003 he created 'The Brake Shop' service for young people with Tourette's Syndrome. By actively modelling how to live a fulfilling, successful life alongside his Tourette's, he helps his young clients both directly and indirectly.

Teacher of the year

More recently, Brad Cohen fulfilled his ambition to become an elementary school teacher despite his TS, even though it took 25 interviews before he got his first job. He went on to be voted Class Teacher of the Year in Georgia, US, and then wrote a book of his experience[13]. This led to him being invited onto *The Oprah Winfrey Show*, and his book was turned into a film first in the US[14] and subsequently as a Bollywood movie in India[15]!

The ticcing surgeon

Perhaps the most remarkable example is Dr Morton Doran, a Canadian surgeon and medical educator who had undiagnosed tics from the age of seven. Undeterred, he fought his way through examinations and graduated from medical school at the age of 24. He then became a GP in rural Canada, specialising in polar medicine (the practice of medicine in isolated settings within extreme cold conditions). He finally realised his diagnosis aged 37, whereupon he joined Canada's Tourette Syndrome Foundation.

Despite his TS diagnosis, he undertook further training and became a surgeon at the age of 39. Subsequently, he was appointed professor of anatomy at the University of Calgary, and to commute from his regular base each week, he obtained a pilot's licence!

TOURETTERS CAN EVEN FLY PLANES! THE TICCING SURGEON

World-renowned neurologist Oliver Sacks was so inspired by Dr Doran's story that he arranged to stay with the surgeon and shadow him in his daily life. Sacks observed that, despite having severe tics, whilst Dr Doran was concentrating on a task such as a surgical procedure, his tics disappeared completely. He also ticced when flying his private plane but was able to control his movements so as not to threaten his safety[16]. Dr Doran finally retired in 2014 and was named a member of the Order of Canada in 2015.

So, to my young survey respondent who said, *"I was planning on becoming a surgeon, but I can't do that anymore" (Elise, 13, US)* – don't give up.

If you can't beat it – stream it!

In the media context, Touretters with more persistent or severe forms are increasingly publicly airing their tic manifestations through online media, partly to raise awareness but also in genuine celebration of the way that tics can be creative, imaginative, and sometimes simply hilarious.

There are young streamers and TikTokkers worldwide with vast followings. Two of the best known from the UK are Sweet Anita and Evie Meg Field aka 'This Trippy Hippie'.

Sweet Anita

In the case of Sweet Anita, despite having tics for many years, she was only formally diagnosed with TS at the age of 24 after she developed coprolalia. She has worked with Tourettes Action hosting fundraisers. She began streaming on Twitch (no pun intended) in 2018 and was named by *Variety* as one of the most influential people in video games in the same year.

Evie Meg Field – This Trippy Hippie

Evie Meg has used her TikTok platform to raise awareness of the challenges of living with Tourette's, especially as a young person. Unlike Sweet Anita, Evie's tics started relatively late in her teens at 15 (she is still only 21 at the time of writing), having previously had a promising career at national level as a champion gymnast (she took part in the Olympic torch relay in 2012). She started on TikTok in 2018 documenting her tics and other mental health challenges, and her following grew exponentially. Recently she has had a book published[17].

Whilst their TS may have prevented them from obtaining 'traditional' jobs, the advent of social media and gaming platforms has provided these young women with not only a means of promoting awareness but also a living, through sponsorship and advertisers.

More and more people are now setting up their own YouTube and TikTok channels. Some of these include:

- **Cece aka 'Otters Have Pockets'** – 18-year-old (in 2022), UK-based, diagnosed with TS in 2020 despite having had tics since the age of five, now a TikTokker with nearly 647,000 followers.
- **Zara Beth aka '@zeezee25'**– UK-based teenage TS advocate on TikTok who documents everyday challenges, including going to restaurants and putting on eye make-up, and her all-time 'viral' classic – attempting a COVID-19 test!
- **Leighton Clarke aka 'Uncle Tics'** – mid-20s Maori New Zealander who works as a videographer both professionally and personally, recording the ups and downs of his life with TS. He is currently followed by 3.9 million people.
- **Glen Cooney aka 'This Tourette's guy'** – a dad in his early 40s from Guernsey in the UK Channel Islands who set up on TikTok, making cookery videos with his wife and young son. In documenting his "epic kitchen fails", his videos highlight his difficulties but are also genuinely funny, and he now has in excess of 4 million followers.

For youngsters with TS, gaining access to these media celebrities as well as smaller-scale chat groups provides a sense of both community and validation, sometimes after years of isolation and misery.

It is hugely encouraging and uplifting to watch young people on YouTube describing their tics as just another part of who they are and laughing about them with fellow Touretters.

Angelica found most of these avenues for herself and enjoys being part of this online community. The key thing for her is that these young media stars are celebrated for who they **are**, *and their followers laugh* **with** *them, not* **at** *them.*

A word of medical caution

Just like the respondents of the teenagers' survey on the Discord server, not all people building a following on online media have received a formal diagnosis of Tourette's. Moreover, some medical professionals have expressed concern that the growth of celebrities putting out videos 'showcasing' their tics may be part of the reason why cases have increased[18].

Voting with their feet

However, the response of young people in the TS population is overwhelmingly positive[19]. They acknowledge that they can 'catch' tics which can sometimes be a problem, but the sense of worldwide community far outweighs any disadvantages.

They are voting with their feet; they want their differences to be 'out there' and for the rest of us 'neurotypicals' to acknowledge and adapt, not the other way round.

Some of the survey respondents put this point across strongly:

"We're just like everyone else, we just have something that slightly sets us apart from people without TS and we should be treated just as someone without TS gets treated." (Elise, 13, US)

> ***"..it does not make us different, and it does not make us unequal" (Grub, 16, UK)***

> ***"It is more common than you think. It does not make us any less capable of achieving goals." (Kathy, 15, US)***

> ***"..it's a spectrum and we are still amazing, wonderful people" (Bailey, 17, Australia)***

This view is well expressed by the Tourette's awareness project **Touretteshero**, set up in 2010 in the UK by Jessica Thom and Matthew Pountney, as a place to "celebrate the humour and creativity of Tourette's". Jess is a theatre-maker and comedian who appeared at the Edinburgh Fringe Festival in 2014 with the first Touretteshero production, *Backstage in Biscuit Land*, and subsequently toured the UK and internationally. Touretteshero works across a variety of creative projects and was awarded an Engagement Fellowship grant by the Wellcome Trust in 2016.

Their strapline is the perfect finishing quote for this book:

'Changing the world one tic at a time'.

Chapter 7: Parent Action Points	
1	Tourette's is not fun to have, but people with Tourette's can have fun. Embrace it with them.
2	Get savvy on TikTok and YouTube (if you aren't already).
3	Encourage your child's dreams and ambitions.

References

Chapter 1

1. Tourette's Disorder, 307.23 (F95.2). Diagnostic and statistical manual of mental disorders: DSM. 5th ed. American Psychiatric Association. 2013. p. 81.

2. Worbe Y, Malherbe C, Hartmann A, Pélégrini-Issac M, Messé A, Vidailhet M et al. Functional immaturity of cortico-basal ganglia networks in Gilles de la Tourette syndrome. Brain. 2012 Jun;135(Pt 6):1937–46. doi:10.1093/brain/aws056. Epub 2012 Mar 19. https://doi.org/10.1093/brain/aws056

3. Cubo E, Galan JMTG, Villaverde VA, Velasco SS, Benito VD, Macarron JV et al. Prevalence of tics in schoolchildren in central Spain: a population-based study. Pediatr Neurol. 2011 Aug;45(2):100–108. https://doi.org/10.1016/j.pediatrneurol.2011.03.003

4. Georgitsi M, Willsey AJ, Mathews CA, State M, Scharf JM, Paschou P. The genetic etiology of Tourette Syndrome: large-scale collaborative efforts on the precipice of discovery. Front Neurosci. 2016 Aug 3. https://doi.org/10.3389/fnins.2016.00351

5. Bitsko RH, Holbrook JR, Visser SN, Mink JW, Zinner SH, Ghandour RM et al. A national profile of Tourette Syndrome, 2011–2012. J Dev Behav Pediatr. 2014;35(5):317–322. Available from: https://pubmed.ncbi.nlm.nih.gov/24906033/

This study concluded that TS was likely to be under-diagnosed, and that the lower prevalence measured in non-white populations might be valid genetic racial differences but might also reflect reduced diagnosis in ethnic minority populations.

6. My life, my story, my Tourette's – The story of one man's life with Tourette's [Documentary film]. Giunta P, director. Ferron D, narrator. USA: Primodio Studios; 2015.

   https://www.youtube.com/watch?v=arjLHxGwNMc
   ...misdiagnosis of Tourette's syndrome as ADHD, especially in Black boys. Chardonde Matthews of Tourette Fellowship at 1.18.25, and Dr Roger Kurlan, Atlantic Neuroscience Institute, USA at 1.18.37....tactile sense of order or symmetry. Dr James Leckman, Yale Medical School, USA, at 32.30.

7. Freeman RD, Zinner SH, Muller-Vahl KR, Fast DK, Burd LJ, Kano Y et al. Coprophenomena in Tourette Syndrome. First published: 19 February 2009 Developmental Medicine & Child Neurology 2009, March;51(3):218-227 Available from: https://doi.org/10.1111/j.1469-8749.2008.03135.x

8. Morris HR, Thacker AJ, Newman PK, Lees AJ. Sign language tics in a prelingually deaf man. Mov Disord. 2000 Mar;15(2):318-20. PMID: 10752584 https://doi.org/10.1002/1531-8257(200003)15:2%3C318::aid-mds1018%3E3.0.co;2-h

9. My F-ing Tourette's family [TV documentary]. Ornbo S, director. Channel 4, UK; 2018.

   ...explaining Tourette's to Eurostar at 25.22.
   ...children ticcing 'Hitler' at German theme park at 42.27.

   https://www.imdb.com/title/tt8365594/

10. Darrow SM, Grados M, Sandor P, Hirschtritt ME, Illmann C, Osiecki L, et al. Autism Spectrum Symptoms in a Tourette's Disorder Sample. J Am Acad Child Adolesc Psychiatry. 2017 Jul;56(7):610-617.e1. Epub 2017 May 11. https://doi.org/10.1016/j.jaac.2017.05.002

Chapter 2

1. My life, my story, my Tourette's – The story of one man's life with Tourette's [Documentary film]. Giunta P, director. Ferron D, narrator. USA: Primodio Studios;2015.https://www.youtube.com/watch?v=arjLHxGwNMc

   Fathers discussing their reaction to son's Tourette's Syndrome diagnosis at 1:04.26.

2. Goetz CG, Leurgans S, Chmura TA. Home alone: methods to maximize tic expression for objective videotape assessments in Gilles de la Tourette syndrome. Movement Disorders. 2001 Jul 17;16(4):693–697. https://doi.org/10.1002/mds.1159

3. Life's a Twitch [Documentary film]. Cindy Bisaillon, director. Canada; 2002. Available from: https://www.nfb.ca/film/lifes_a_twitch/

Chapter 3

1. Tourette Syndrome (UK) Assocation [Internet]. Hampshire (UK). Tourettes Action website. Available from: https://www.tourettes-action.org.uk/85-health-professionals.html

2. Mol Debes NM, Hjalgrim H, Skov L. Limited knowledge of Tourette syndrome causes delay in diagnosis.

Neuropediatrics. 2008 Apr;39(2):101–105. https://doi.org/10.1055/s-2008-1081457

3. Turner, C. 'Explosion' of children with tics and Tourette's from lockdown. The Telegraph. 2021 Feb 13. Available from: https://www.telegraph.co.uk/news/2021/02/13/explosion-children-tics-tourettes-lockdown/

4. Heyman I, Liang H, Hedderly T. COVID-19 related increase in childhood tics and tic-like attacks. Arch Dis Child. 2021;106(5). *Free* http://dx.doi.org/10.1136/archdischild-2021-321748

5. Conte G, Baglioni V, Valente F, Chiarotti F, Cardona F. Adverse mental health impact of the COVID-19 lockdown in individuals with Tourette syndrome in Italy: an online survey. Front Psychiatry. 30 November 2020;11:583744. https://doi.org/10.3389/fpsyt.2020.583744

6. YoungMinds website quoting Health Service Journal, 2018 https://www.youngminds.org.uk/

7. Hansen AS, Telleus GK, Mohr-Jensen C, Lauritsen MB. Parent-perceived barriers to accessing services for their child's mental health problems. Child Adolesc Psychiatry Ment Health. 2021;15(Article 4). https://doi.org/10.1186/s13034-021-00357-7

8. Capriotti MR, Himle MB, Woods DW. Behavioral Treatments for Tourette Syndrome. J. Obsessive Compuls Relat Disord. 2014 Oct;3(4):415–420. doi.org/10.1016/j.jocrd.2014.03.007. J Obsessive Compuls Relat Disord. 2014 Oct; 3(4): 415–420.

9. Azrin NH, Nunn RG. Habit-reversal: a method of eliminating nervous habits and tics. Behav Res Ther. 1973 Nov;11(4):619–28. https://doi.org/10.1016/0005-7967(73)90119-8

10. Woods DW, Piacentini J, Chang S, Deckersbach T, Ginsburg G, Peterson A et al. Managing Tourette Syndrome: a behavioural intervention for children and adults. Oxford University Press; 2008. https://www.amazon.co.uk/Managing-Tourette-Syndrome-Behavioral-Intervention-ebook/dp/B001Y35GGU

11. https://www.tourettes-action.org.uk/71-behavioural-therapies.html

12. https://tourette.org/research-medical/cbit-overview/

13. Whittington C, Pennant M, Kendall T, Glazebrook C, Trayner P, Groom M et al. Practitioner review: Treatments for Tourette syndrome in children and young people – a systematic review. J Child Psychol Psychiatr. 2016;57:988–1004. https://doi.org/10.1111/jcpp.12556

14. Blakemore S-J. The mysterious workings of the adolescent brain [Internet]. 2012. Video: 14:10. Available from: https://www.ted.com/talks/sarah_jayne_blakemore_the_mysterious_workings_of_the_adolescent_brain

    Sarah-Jayne Blakemore is a brilliant UK-based neuroscientist who has published widely. Her TED talk from 2012 is both fascinating and accessible.

15. The Institute of Mental Health [Internet]. Nottingham (UK). What is ORBIT? Available from: https://www.institutemh.org.uk/research/projects-and-studies/current-studies/orbit/199-what-is-orbit

16. Hollis C, Hall CL, Jones R, Marston L, Le Novere M, Hunter R et al. Therapist-supported online remote behavioural intervention for tics in children and adolescents in England (ORBIT): a

multicentre, parallel group, single-blind, randomised controlled trial. Lancet Psychiatry 2021;8: 871-82 https://doi.org/10.1016/S2215-0366(21)00235-2

17. Martinez-Ramirez D, Jimenez-Shahed J, Leckman JF, Porta M, Servello D, Meng F-G et al. Efficacy and safety of deep brain stimulation in Tourette Syndrome. The International Tourette Syndrome Deep Brain Stimulation Public Database and Registry. JAMA Neurol. 2018;75(3):353–359. https://doi.org/10.1001/jamaneurol.2017.4317

18. Morera Maiquez B, Sigurdsson HP, Dyke K, Clarke E, McGrath P, Pasche M et al. Entraining movement-related brain oscillations to suppress tics in Tourette Syndrome. Curr Biol. 2020 Jun 22;30(12)2334–2342.e3. Epub 2020 Jun 4. https://doi.org/10.1016/j.cub.2020.04.044

Chapter 4

1. Otters Have Pockets. What I'd like teachers to know about Tourette's Syndrome. YouTube April 3, 2021 https://www.youtube.com/watch?v=Vdf7aB2hmo8

2. Eapen V, Cavanna AE, Robertson MM. Comorbidities, social impact, and quality of life in Tourette Syndrome. Front Psychiatry. 2016 Jun 6;7:97. https://doi.org/10.3389/fpsyt.2016.00097

3. BBC Bitesize [Internet]. UK. Millennials, baby boomers or Gen Z: Which one are you and what does it mean? Available from: https://www.bbc.co.uk/bitesize/articles/zf8j92p

Chapter 5

1. Eapen V, Črnčec R, McPherson S, Snedden C. Tic disorders and learning disability: clinical characteristics, cognitive performance and comorbidity. Australas J Spec Educ. 2013;37(2):162–72. https://doi.org/10.1017/jse.2013.2

2. Mitchell JW, Cavanna AE [Letter]. Handwriting abnormality in Tourette Syndrome. J Neuropsychiatry Clin Neurosci. 2013 Apr 1. https://doi.org/10.1176/appi.neuropsych.12050116

3. Lord Baker (former UK Secretary of State for Education). Symposium held by the Royal Society of Medicine, April 2021. https://www.rsm.ac.uk/latest-news/2021/education-in-the-time-of-covid/

4. NHS Digital. UK. Mental health of children and young people in England, 2020: Wave 1 follow up to the 2017 survey. 2020 Oct 22. Available from: https://digital.nhs.uk/data-and-information/publications/statistical/mental-health-of-children-and-young-people-in-england/2020-wave-1-follow-up

Chapter 6

1. Wadman R, Tischler V, Jackson GM. Everybody just thinks I'm weird: a qualitative exploration of the psychosocial experiences of adolescents with Tourette syndrome. Child Care Health Dev. 2013 Nov;39(6):880–6. Epub 2013 Jan 30 https://doi.org/10.1111/cch.12033

2. Alwani E. What it's like to have Tourette's – and how music gives me back control [Internet]. 2019. Video: 09:47. Available from: https://www.ted.com/talks/esha_alwani_what_it_s_like_to_have_tourette_s_and_how_music_gives_me_back_control

3. Teenage tics [TV documentary]. Clough M, director. BBC TV; 2017.

https://www.youtube.com/watch?v=70ydMtRfSPc

...Greg Storey at 11.46.

...Meeting community police officers at 13:00.

4. Collicott NJ, Stern JS, Williams D, Grabecki K, Simmons H, Robertson MM. Tic attacks in Tourette Syndrome. Association of British Neurologists (ABN) joint meeting with the Royal College of Physicians (RCP). London, 23–24 October 2013. JNeurolNeurosurgPsychiatry.2013;84(11). https://jnnp.bmj.com/content/84/11/e2.77

5. Dragons' Den – *a BBC TV reality show in which aspiring entrepreneurs 'pitch' their product to a panel of established, successful businesspeople. If sufficiently impressed, the 'Dragons' can choose to offer a funding or partnership deal. The format is owned by Sony Pictures Television, based on the original Japanese programme, which has been sold worldwide. The UK version has been running since 2005.*

6. Rae CL, Polyanska L, Gould van Praag CD, Parkinson J, Bouyagoub S, Nagai Y et al. Face perception enhances insula and motor network reactivity in Tourette syndrome.Brain.2018 Nov;141(11):3249–3261. https://doi.org/10.1093/brain/awy254

7. Unwin D, director. Horrid Henry eats out [TV series]. Horrid Henry, series 1, episode 15, Novel Entertainment (UK). Aired 2007 Feb 20. *Based on books by Francesca Simon.* https://www.youtube.com/watch?v=iKBhNgZ8C_I

Chapter 7

1. Higgins LD, Nielsen ME. Responding to the needs of twice-exceptional learners: a school district and university's collaborative approach. In: Kay K, editor. Uniquely gifted: Identifying and meeting the needs of the twice-exceptional student. Gilsum, NH: Avocus Publishing; 2000. p. 287–303.

2. Mueller SC, Jackson GM, Dhalla R, Datsopoulos S, Hollis CP. Enhanced cognitive control in young people with Tourette's syndrome. Curr Biol. 2006 Mar;16(6):570–3. doi:10.1016/j.cub.2006.01.064. PMID 16546080.

3. Dye CD, Walenski M, Mostofsky SH, Ullman MT. A verbal strength in children with Tourette syndrome? Evidence from a non-word repetition task. Brain Lang. 2016 Sep;160:61-70. doi: 10.1016/j.bandl.2016.07.005. Epub 2016 Aug 1. PMID: 27479738. https://pubmed.ncbi.nlm.nih.gov/27479738/

4. Colautti L, Magenes S, Rago S, Zanaboni Dina C, Cancer A, Antonietti A. Creative thinking in Tourette's Syndrome: An uncharted topic. Front Psychol. 2021 Apr 22;12:649814 https://doi.org/10.3389/fpsyg.2021.649814

5. Teenage tics [TV documentary]. Clough M, director. BBC TV; 2017 at 22:00.https://www.youtube.com/watch?v=70ydMtRfSPc

6. MrGregles [Internet]. Available from: https://www.mrgregles.com

7. Big Brother (British TV series) Channel 4; 2000–2010. *British version of the international reality television franchise Big Brother created by producer John de Mol in 1997.*

8. Ashoori A, Jankovic J. Mozart's movements and behaviour: a

case of Tourette's syndrome? J Neurol Neurosurg Psychiatry. 2007 Nov;78(11):1171–5. doi:10.1136/jnnp.2007.114520. https://pubmed.ncbi.nlm.nih.gov/17940168/

9. Pearce JM. Doctor Samuel Johnson: 'the great convulsionary' a victim of Gilles de la Tourette's syndrome. J R Soc Med. 1994 Jul;87(7):396–9. https://pubmed.ncbi.nlm.nih.gov/8046726/

10. Coren G. Yes of course these tics are blinking annoying. The Times. 2021 Mar 26. https://www.thetimes.co.uk/article/yes-of-course-these-tics-are-blinking-annoying-39ppsj9ck

11. Meyer C. Free Expression/Polly Draper drew on her husband's Tourette's syndrome for 'The Tic Code' [Internet]. SFGATE. 2000 Aug 30. Available from: https://www.sfgate.com/entertainment/article/Free-Expression-Polly-Draper-drew-on-her-3238511.php

12. McKinlay BD. Nix Your Tics! Eliminate Unwanted Tic Symptoms. Life's a Twitch! Publishing; 2015. http://www.lifesatwitch.com/nixyourtics_book.html

13. Cohen B. Front of the Class: How Tourette Syndrome Made Me the Teacher I Never Had. Macmillan; 2009. https://www.amazon.co.uk/Front-Class-Brad-Cohen/dp/0312571399

14. Front of the class [TV film]. Werner P, director. McGee Productions; 2008. https://www.youtube.com/watch?v=hP7R61y_Rfk

15. Hichki [Film]. Malhotra SP, director. Yash Raj Films; 2018. https://www.youtube.com/watch?v=rnEFeXvGszc

16. Sacks O. A surgeon's life. In: An Anthropologist on Mars: Seven Paradoxical Tales. New York: Vintage Books. 1995.

17. Meg E (aka This Trippy Hippie). My Nonidentical Twin: One Ordinary Girl. One Life-Changing Condition. How Tourette's Changes Your World. Little, Brown Book Group; 2021.

18. Olvera C, Stebbins GT, Goetz CG, Kompoliti K. TikTok tics: a pandemic within a pandemic. Mov Disord. 2021 Jul 28. https://doi.org/10.1002/mdc3.13316

19. Perkins V, Coulson NS, Davies EB. Using online support communities for Tourette Syndrome and tic disorders: Online survey of users' experiences. J Med Internet Res2020;22(11):e18099.doi:10.2196/18099. PMID:33141089;PMCID:PMC7671842 https://pubmed.ncbi.nlm.nih.gov/33141089/

Additional Resources

National and regional charities

UK

Tourettes Action (Tourette Syndrome (UK) Association): https// www.tourettes-action.org.uk – excellent website with a great deal of information; includes video presentations for schools and practical tools such as the TA Passport for young people to take into schools. Also lists regional parent support groups.

Tourette Alliance: http://tourettealliance.org (Northern Ireland)

Tourette Scotland: https://www.tourettescotland.org

North America and Canada

Tourette Association of America: https://tourette.org – has links to individual state support groups

Tourette Canada: https://tourette.ca

Australia

Tourette Syndrome Association of Australia Inc: https://tourette.org.au/

Europe and World

If you are in another country than those listed above, visit the Tourettes Action website – https//www.tourettes-action.org.uk

– as they list all the currently known Tourette's associations worldwide.

Other websites of interest

Tourettesheroe: https://www.touretteshero.com

One final thing

If you liked this book, and feel that it has helped you, I would be very grateful if you could spare the time to leave a review on Amazon, please.

You can drop me a line or ask me questions by emailing me at:

mandy@comptongray.com

I'd love to get the word out there to everyone who could benefit from reading this book and I would really appreciate any help you could give with this.

- Let me know if you have other ideas for additions to a possible later edition of this book
- Send me photos of you with my book (if you're happy for me to feature them in promotional material)
- Point me towards any podcast interviewers or journalists who may be interested in promoting this book

Manufactured by Amazon.ca
Acheson, AB